£3.50

I WANT TO BE A CHURCH MEMBER

I WANT TO BE A CHURCH MEMBER

G. Eric Lane

EVANGELICAL PRESS OF WALES

© Evangelical Press of Wales, 1992
First edition, 1992
ISBN 1 85049 101 1

All rights reserved. No part of this publication may be reproduced, stored in a retrieval system, or transmitted, in any form or by any means, electronic, mechanical, photo-copying, recording or otherwise, without the prior permission of the Evangelical Press of Wales.

Cover design: Cain Graphics, Rhiain M. Davies

Scripture quotations taken from
the *Holy Bible, New International Version.*
Copyright © 1973, 1978, 1984 by International Bible Society.
Used by permission of Hodder and Stoughton Limited.

Published by the Evangelical Press of Wales
Bryntirion, Bridgend, Mid Glamorgan, CF31 4DX, Wales
Printed in Wales by WBC Print Ltd, Bridgend

Contents

Introduction: Becoming a church member	7
1. Why join a local church?	9
2. Who is eligible to join a local church?	22
3. What is the procedure for joining a church?	37
4. How is a new member received?	48
5. What am I committing myself to?	57
6. Who leads the church?	71
7. Who assists the elders?	87
8. How does church membership end?	94
9. Is there life outside the local church?	104

To the members of Westhoughton Evangelical Church, Lancashire, for whom the material used in this book was originally prepared.

Introduction:
BECOMING A CHURCH MEMBER

This book is written primarily for those who have recently become Christians. Most Christians come to faith in Christ either through attending a local church or through the witness of a friend who belongs to a local church. This is probably true of you. If it is, you will remember how wonderful it was to discover what Christianity is all about, and how you rejoiced to know that Jesus had saved you. Since that time you have been attending a church and growing in grace and the knowledge of God.

In case anyone reading this book has not yet become attached to a local church, let me stress the importance of doing so. When God became your Father through your faith in Jesus, all other Christians became your brothers and sisters. God's purpose in salvation was not just to bring individuals to himself but to set up a family – a great world-wide spiritual family and particular families in local communities. Our western culture is very individualistic, but the part of the world to which Jesus came thought in terms of communities. This was true in Israel and continued from the beginning of the gospel. Those who believed came together for fellowship, instruction and worship (Acts 2:42). Everywhere the gospel was preached and people believed, churches were planted. It was and is through churches that people come to know our Saviour now.

You need a local church and a local church needs you and your contribution. Resist the temptation to rotate round a number of different churches. You cannot establish close ties if your attendance is irregular, nor can you make a helpful contribution to the church's activities. It is not always easy to find a nearby church which preaches the same gospel through which you were saved. If there is not such a church in your community, you may have to travel to find one. You will not be the first to do so. Who knows but that in the process of time others in your community may become Christians and a new church planted? This has happened many times. God must have had a purpose in bringing you to himself knowing there was no gospel church near you. If there are difficulties about your choice, consult the person or persons most instrumental in your conversion. If you still feel unenthusiastic on the matter go on reading and it may all become clearer! For now we will take it you are at least in the process of settling into regular attendance in a gospel church.

You have now come to the point when you are beginning to think not just about your relationship with God but with the church you are attending. Probably you will have heard that most of the people are called 'members'. You may be wondering what this means and why you aren't a member. Do you need to be a member? If so, you would like to know how you become a member and what is involved.

The answers to these questions and many others are in the New Testament. They are not as clear and obvious as the answer to the question, 'What must I do to be saved?', because that question is so much more important. Nevertheless, church membership is there, although we have to do some spadework to clarify it.

The following chapters look at a number of questions about church membership and seek to answer them by referring to the appropriate passages in the Bible.

1
WHY JOIN A LOCAL CHURCH?

This is the first question you will want answered. You will want to be persuaded from Scripture that, having come to Jesus in faith and professed him in baptism, you need to do something more. You cannot see why you should seek membership just because it seems the thing to do. This is a healthy approach. Even evangelical churches have built their human traditions on to their divine foundations without warrant and thereby produced a deadness over the years. If we cannot make a case for membership from Scripture then we should give up the whole idea.

The very fact that you and others have a query here indicates that there is a genuine problem. The case for membership is not as clear-cut as that for personal conversion or even baptism. There are no simple proof-texts we can point to which say, 'Join the church', as there are which say, 'Believe on the Lord Jesus Christ', or 'Repent and be baptized'.

In a way this need not worry or even surprise us. Church membership is not essential in the way faith in Christ is. Joining a church will not make us any more saved than we were before. Non-members who are believers are no less precious in the Lord's eyes than those who are members. Heaven is no more sure for the latter than the former. The main thrust of the Bible is to bring us to faith in Christ. About this there must be no trace of doubt, whatever else is left obscure. On some matters there is room for debate, but not on the way of salvation. So do not be surprised if

I want to be a church member

you cannot see membership as clearly as you can salvation. Not all things in Scripture are presented with the same degree of dogmatism.

On the other hand all things in the Bible are equally true because they have all come from the mind of the same God (2 Timothy 3:16). That is why they are all 'useful'. A believer who wants to be fully mature, 'thoroughly equipped for every good work' (2 Timothy 3:17), will want to be obedient in everything it teaches. This will include membership of the local church.

To say 'there are no simple proof-texts we can point to' on church membership does not mean to say that there are no relevant verses or passages on the subject. What it means is that church membership is not the main subject of these scriptures. Nevertheless it is there, either as a secondary subject or by implication. Take, for example, what Paul says about a church gathering in 1 Corinthians 14:23-25. 'The whole church comes together' for worship and ministry. Sometimes 'unbelievers' attend or 'some who do not understand'. This latter group clearly refers to people who cannot be classed either as 'the church' or as 'unbelievers'. The word used to describe them is literally 'uninstructed' and refers to people who are interested in the gospel, attracted to it, and even seeking salvation, but not yet committed. These are distinguished from 'the church', which is a clearly defined group – or as we would put it, from the members of the church.

A similar distinction is found earlier in the letter in 5:12-13, where Paul speaks of those 'outside the church' and 'those inside'. You will notice that he does not define the difference in terms of their relationship to Christ but to the church. We would call them 'members' and 'non-members'.

Interesting, you say, but is that all there is? These odd words and phrases are not enough to persuade me to take

Why join a local church?

a step as important as joining a church! Quite right. They are only pointers, straws in the wind. The main arguments have a much more solid basis. They all have to do with the fact that our faith in Christ brings us into a relationship not only with God but with other Christians. The New Testament has a great deal to say about this relationship. We can see this and its bearing on church membership in a number of ways.

1. *We can see it in the way the church and churches of Christ began*

Turn to Matthew 16:13-20.

Since the word 'church' (from the Greek *kuriakos*) means 'belonging to the Lord' it applies to all God's people in any age. It applies to the people of Israel before the coming of Jesus, who were a 'congregation' of God's people and therefore a church. Jesus here, however, was obviously making a new start: 'I will build my church.' It was to be his own personal church ('my') and its completion still lay in the future ('will build'). Although Peter and the other disciples were Jews and thus of the congregation of Israel, they did not belong to the church of Jesus until this occasion at Caesarea Philippi. Something happened there and then which brought them into his church.

It all centred in Simon, although he was evidently speaking on behalf of all the others. In answer to Jesus' question, 'Who do you say I am?' (v.15), Simon stated, 'You are the Christ, the Son of the living God' (v.16). In saying this he was not prompted by someone else, but moved by God who had revealed it to him (v.17). Jesus immediately began to speak to him about his church (v.18). This church he was about to bring into being would be like a building, and the foundation stone was to be the open confession of faith in himself. Because Peter was the first to

I want to be a church member

make this confession he would be the first 'stone' in the building. This is why Jesus gave him the name for which he is better known: 'Peter', which means 'a stone'. So it does not refer to strength of character – in fact Peter was very volatile – but to his place in the church.

Immediately after this Jesus gave the twelve apostles authority to go and establish churches all over the world (v.19) until he had a whole 'kingdom' of them. Giving them 'the keys' meant that they would have the privilege of teaching and governing these churches on his behalf. This was not to start immediately, however. For the time being they must restrain themselves (v.20).

The message to us is clear. As soon as the Lord God has opened our understanding to see Jesus as his Son and our Saviour, as soon as we have come to faith in him, we become the stones out of which he builds his church. We have the authority of Peter himself, the first stone, for this: 'as you come to him, the living Stone . . . you also, like living stones, are being built into a spiritual house' (1 Peter 2:4-5). Stones, once quarried and shaped, are fitted into the building. This is what church membership is – it is you taking your place in the company for which God has prepared you. Coming to faith in Christ brings you, not just to God, but to other believers. You need to be slotted into your place among them. If that was so at the beginning, should it not be so right through time?

2. *We can see it in the way the apostles discharged their commission*

It would help to have the Acts of the Apostles open in front of you.

We saw just now that although Jesus authorized them for the work of his kingdom, he delayed the actual execution of the work. They were not ready and neither was he.

Why join a local church?

First he must die to purchase all his people and make them God's possession. Then he must rise from the dead to assume power over all created things, material and spiritual. It was when he had achieved these things that he came to the apostles again and commissioned them to 'go and make disciples of all nations, baptising them ... and teaching them ...' (Matthew 28:18-20). Some days later the Holy Spirit came upon them (Acts 2) and they were given the necessary powers of understanding and boldness to begin carrying out this charge to be 'witnesses', just as Jesus promised in his last words before leaving them (Acts 1:8).

The rest of the book of Acts describes how these men discharged their commission. It is a thrilling story. Read it for yourself. It begins in Jerusalem, where the apostles, after receiving the Holy Spirit, immediately preached Jesus as Messiah and Son of God (Acts 2:36). Many believed and openly confessed their faith (v.41) just as the Twelve had done at Caesarea Philippi. These new stones were then fitted into the building, the church in Jerusalem (vv.41-47).

What had happened in Jerusalem later happened in Samaria when a man called Philip 'proclaimed the Christ' (8:5). Again, many believed (v.12) and so a church came into being in Samaria (9:31). In a similar way a church came into being in far away Ethiopia, because Philip preached Jesus to its Chancellor of the Exchequer as he travelled in his chariot, so that he returned home a believer (8:26-39). Philip's witness led to churches springing up all along the Mediterranean coast (8:40), in places such as Joppa (9:36), Phoenicia (11:19), Tyre (21:3-4), Ptolemais (21:7) and Caesarea (21:8). Through other Christians who were forced out of Jerusalem by persecution (8:1) churches came into being in the towns of Syria, such as Damascus (9:1-2) and Antioch (11:19-26).

I want to be a church member

Through Paul's successful preaching of Jesus as Christ, churches came into being in his own province of Cilicia (15:23,41), the vast Roman district of Galatia (chapters 13-14), Macedonia on the continent of Europe (chapters 16-17), Achaia, which is modern Greece (chapters 17-18), other parts of Asia Minor or, as we know it, Turkey (chapters 18-19), and possibly even Spain (Romans 15:28). Churches were also set up in the Black Sea area – perhaps even by Peter himself (1 Peter 1:1).

So we could go on. The point is that every time Jesus was preached, people believed and owned him publicly, so that another church came into being. The church you attend is there for exactly the same reason. At some time in the distant or recent past somebody came to your community and preached that Jesus is Lord. A number believed, confessed their faith and formed a church. Later, more believed and were 'added to their number', just as at the very beginning (Acts 2:41). You yourself are one of the most recent to respond. Why break the golden chain by standing aloof from the others? You have already come into an invisible or spiritual relationship with them by the very fact of believing in the same Jesus. Why not make the relationship visible? You *are* a stone; why not let yourself be slotted into place by becoming a member? It has been going on for two thousand years! Why not continue? It is not an evangelical tradition of recent date. It began when the kingdom itself began.

Still not convinced? Think of it as like marriage. You fall in love with someone and commit yourself to that person. But before you consummate that love by living together, you regularize it publicly in marriage. It is the same in this matter. In your baptism you declared that you belong to Christ, you love him. Now declare you belong to his people, his 'building', by becoming a member of your local church.

3. We can see it in the way the apostles wrote about the relationship between Christians

Ephesians 4:1-16 is important here.

In the first three chapters of Ephesians Paul has thrilled us with a vision of all the spiritual riches we have inherited through faith in Christ. Now he calls us to learn to live in the light of them, or as he puts it in verse 1, to 'live a life worthy of the calling you have received'. The interesting thing is that he immediately goes on to talk about qualities that have to do with how we relate to the other believers in the local church. We are to be humble, gentle and patient with each other (v.2). We are to make every effort to keep the church 'one' (v.3). It is not enough to have a common basis of faith (vv.4-6). There must also be a 'bond of peace' (v.3).

These are things we have to work at – 'make every effort' (v.3). Why? Because when we become Christians we do not lose our individual personality, we do not all become the same. God forbid that we should! How monotonous the Christian scene would be if we were all exactly alike in the church! Variety and diversity are one of God's most marvellous ideas and achievements. No two snowflakes are identical, neither are two people. Even twins said to be identical physically have different personalities. We do not lose this individuality when we become Christians. Peter, John and Paul were all different from each other – just as much after conversion as before. In fact, we could say – more different. For the new birth awakens gifts, graces and abilities which were only dormant before. Also it channels gifts previously exercised into new and more profitable directions in the service of the Lord. So with us all.

These differences mean we have to work hard to fit in with the others in the church. We must avoid the temptation to form parties and cliques based on personality or

I want to be a church member

ability. Rather we must use our distinct characteristics and gifts to complement what is lacking in others. This is what Paul is teaching in Ephesians 4. In verse 8 he says that Christ has poured on his church an abundance of gifts, which he has distributed among the individual believers. It is the responsibility of each one of us to use these for the good of all, so that the church becomes more and more united (vv.13-16).

This is where church membership comes in, for church membership is accepting this principle of unity in diversity and pledging ourselves to work for its improvement. Diversity in unity is the keynote of the church; and coming into conscious committed membership is the way we recognize it, glory in it and dedicate ourselves to its advancement. Church membership is what enables the church to function along these lines.

4. We can see it in the illustrations the apostles use to give us a full and vivid picture of a church

There is nothing like a picture to attract us! Where shall I go for my holiday? The Lakes? Cornwall? Greece? These are just names. It is when I see a picture that I make up my mind. I am the dupe of the travel brochure! The New Testament letters are God's travel brochures, to entice us into membership. The words 'church membership' or 'join the church' sound dull and formal. They are just words. So the Lord shows us they are really glorious experiences. He gives us four different views.

The first is a view of a beautiful building

This was the way Jesus put it to Peter at Caesarea Philippi (Matthew 16:18). Peter himself echoed this in his first letter (2:4-5). Paul used the same picture in Ephesians

2:19-22. They are probably thinking of the Temple in Jerusalem. The original one, built by Solomon, was a building of great beauty because of its classical proportions. Read Psalm 48 to see its effect on one visitor. It had been destroyed in the Babylonian conquest and rebuilt on a smaller scale after the exile. Herod spent many years enlarging it and embellishing it, making it something to marvel at again, as the disciples did when they saw it (Mark 13:1).

Jesus, however, said it would be destroyed, in spite of its great beauty and its special place in God's purposes. The Temple existed not so much that its architecture might be admired as that its God might be glorified. In the same way the cathedrals of Europe were built as a way of exalting the Lord and showing his splendours. If buildings could really do this, these would. In fact, God no longer requires buildings either to dwell in or to show off his beauty. The believers in Jesus are his temple. Paul told the Corinthians they were 'God's building': 'Don't you know that you yourselves are God's temple?' (1 Corinthians 3:9,16). To the Ephesians he wrote: 'You are . . . built on the foundation of the apostles and prophets, with Christ Jesus himself as the chief corner-stone. In him the whole building is joined together and rises to become a holy temple in the Lord' (Ephesians 2:19-21). So Jesus dwells among his believing people, they worship him together with heart and voice and glorify him by their lives.

To do this they must be built together. Saving faith makes us like precious stones, each one beautiful in its own way. But membership fits us together into a unified structure which we call a building. Stones are of different shapes, sizes, colours and materials. The builder fits them together and gives them a beauty exceeding the sum total of their individual parts. Each of us is different in character and gifts. Christ's salvation sanctifies our particular personality and makes each of us a precious stone. Building us into a church creates a beauty beyond that of each individual. Just as your favourite cathedral is much more beautiful than a scattering of separate pieces of stone, wood, metal or glass, however well shaped each one is, so is a church much more glorious than a number of isolated, individual Christians, however gifted or holy each one may be.

On top is Jesus himself, 'the chief corner-stone', like the pinnacle of the Temple or the soaring spire of the cathedral. You must want to be in on this! That is what church membership does.

The second is a view of the human body

Paul loved using this picture of a church. It comes in Ephesians 4:12-16 and at greater length in 1 Corinthians 12. How lovely the human body is! Christians need have no hang-ups about it. There is nothing disgusting about a painting of a nude or indecent about ballet dancing. Of course, these things, like the body itself, are easily abused, but the fact remains that God made the human body in his image, both male and female, and endued it with something reflecting his own beauty in its form and movement. The church is the body of his Son – not as it was when 'he had no beauty or majesty to attract us to him' (Isaiah 53:2), but as it became when he ascended and was glorified, a body such as John attempts to describe in Revelation 1.

Nor is it just its form that makes the body an object of wonder. Think of its vast variety of functions and all the parts God made to perform these. Then think of how they are all connected: by joints, ligaments and nerves, with blood and brain cells animating them all. No wonder Shakespeare wrote:

Why join a local church?

> What a piece of work is a man! How noble in reason! how infinite in faculty! in form, in moving, how express and admirable! in action how like an angel! in apprehension how like a god! the beauty of the world! the paragon of animals! (*Hamlet*, II.ii.323-328).

The church is the body beautiful. It has many 'members' or 'parts' – you and I. Each of us has our particular contribution to make to its operation. When we are all functioning in harmony we are the body of Christ, the perfect Son of God, lovely in form and graceful in movement. What beauty is there in an organ severed from the body, and what use is it? It is the joining together, the membership, that makes it a body. By joining a church you enhance its beauty and assist its functioning.

The third is a view of a flock of sheep

Jesus spoke of himself as the shepherd and his disciples as sheep (John 10). He used a picture which came first to the mind of David (Psalm 23). The apostles took it up, although perhaps not with the same enthusiasm as they did the first two pictures (1 Peter 5:1-4). In the ancient world flocks of animals were objects of great beauty. The lover in the Song of Solomon describes his beloved's hair as 'like a flock of goats descending from Mount Gilead' and her teeth as 'like a flock of sheep just shorn, coming up from the washing' (Song 4:1-2). This probably tells us more about how much the ancients valued their animals than it does about how Solomon admired his beloved! Even in modern industrial Britain there is still something captivating about sheep grazing in a green field or on a mountainside.

Moreover, the shepherd becomes very attached to his sheep in spite of their aggravating ways. This is probably because they are so dependent on him – for food, shelter, guidance and safety. No doubt this was why Jesus used the illustration. It is the other side of the previous picture. We are clever and useful like the parts of a body; but apart from Christ we are as useless as sheep without a shepherd. We absolutely depend on him. Yet there is something appealing even about dependence. The helpless baby, the kitten, and the lamb all strike our hearts. When you become a church member you are saying, 'I can't make it alone – I need the flock, I need the shepherd.' The shepherd is always found where the flock is (Song 1:7-8). Only rarely is he out in the mountains on his own, and that is when he is searching for a lost sheep. Otherwise he is always with the flock. This is why Jesus said, 'Where two or three come together in my name, there am I with them' (Matthew 18:20). If you want to know where to find Jesus, look for some of his sheep – he is sure to be among them! Church membership is being in the flock feeding in the green pasture and drinking from the still water to which the shepherd has led them.

The fourth is a view of the family
When Jesus at the beginning of his ministry taught his disciples to pray to God as 'Our Father' (Matthew 6:9), he was telling us something not only about our new relationship with God but also with each other. If God is Father of each one who believes in Jesus, then together we form his family. This was how he tried to get his disciples to regard each other (Mark 3:33-34). This was the basis of his appeal to them to love each other, as it was that of his disciples later (Hebrews 13:1; 1 John 5:1).

The family is the basic unit of human life as created by God. You cannot break it up without society disintegrating. Everyone enjoys being with or part of a family that is bound by love. Everyone grieves over the hurt that marks a divided or broken family. Everyone needs to feel part of a

Why join a local church?

family. A lone Christian is a lonely Christian. Church membership is being welcomed into the bosom of the family of which God is Father and Jesus the elder brother.

God has given us four pictures of the church, not one. This is not just to emphasize and prove the point by repetition, but also to say four different things about what it means to be a member of a church. To be a stone in his temple means to belong to a worshipping community. To be part of a body means to belong to a living, functioning, serving, witnessing community. To be a sheep in the flock means belonging to a community dependent on him for food, protection and direction. To be a member of a family is to belong to a community bound by a common fatherhood. Put together you have the main functions of an individual Christian. Evidently we are meant to fulfil these not on our own but together in the church. Now can you see the answer to the question why you should join a church?

2
WHO IS ELIGIBLE TO JOIN A LOCAL CHURCH?

Can any Christian become a member of a local church? Does it matter how long or short a time I have been a Christian? Do I have to wait until I reach a certain standard? Do I have to undergo other spiritual experiences after conversion? Do I have to undertake a course of instruction and pass an examination? What are the qualifications for church membership?

This is a problem that has vexed churches down the ages. At some periods churches have been too restrictive and imposed too many conditions. The result of this was often to divide the believers in the congregation into two groups – those who were members and those who were not, who sometimes formed the majority. Others have been too lax and admitted anyone expressing a desire for membership, even those quite unclear about their spiritual standing. This latter was the position that the great Jonathan Edwards found when he became pastor of the church in Northampton, Massachusetts in the eighteenth century. So automatic was the procedure for admitting members that the nominal members greatly outnumbered those who had made a clear personal commitment to Jesus Christ. Edwards came to the view that a definite profession of personal conversion should be required for membership. But when he sought to implement this view it cost him his position.

There is no need for this aspect of our subject to be a problem or a bone of contention, if we work it out from the material we have considered in Chapter 1. In that chapter we thought first about how the local church originated. We looked at what happened at the place where it all began – Caesarea Philippi, where Jesus declared Peter to be the first 'stone' in the new church he was building. Next we went on to see how the apostles went about planting churches wherever they preached the gospel. Every passage we considered led us to the same conclusion: a local church comes into being when the gospel of Christ is preached and some of the hearers believe it in their hearts and confess it with their mouths. This was what Peter and the other apostles did at Caesarea Philippi, and it was what they called on others to do when they took over from Jesus at Pentecost. Those who responded to their message became the members of the churches which came into existence.

Then we went a stage further and saw how this faith which responds to the call of Christ and brings us into a relationship with him also bring us into a close spiritual relationship with others who have responded in a similar way. This relationship exists whether the others came to faith at the same time and in the same place as ourselves or years before in some other place. In becoming members we are simply acknowledging the existence of this relationship and accepting the obligations that follow. In a spiritual sense we become 'joined' to them when by faith we acknowledge the same Saviour and Lord as they. Becoming members means recognizing that formally and openly.

Finally, by studying four pictures drawn by God in his Word, we saw what the local church is for, what it can be or do that each of us would find impossible on his own. The four pictures bring out four aspects of this. The first was that of a building comprising a number of separate stones which, when arranged together, form a 'temple', a place of worship. This showed us the church as a worshipping community. The question is, 'How do I become a stone?' and the answer is the way Peter did, by confessing faith in Jesus as the Christ, the Lord and Saviour. As Peter himself later wrote: 'As you come to him, the living Stone . . . you also, like living stones, are being built into a spiritual house' (1 Peter 2:4-5). The relevant words are 'as you come to him', that is, as you by faith own him as your Saviour and God.

The church is also like a body, composed of many different parts which together make an organic whole. Each part has its contribution to make for the good of all the others and the whole body. How do we become a part of this body? Paul's most extended treatment of this illustration in 1 Corinthians 12 begins by saying, 'No-one can say, "Jesus is Lord," except by the Holy Spirit' (v.3). This again is just what Peter and the other apostles did at Caesarea Philippi, and what they called on others to do when they preached, that is, to own Jesus as Lord. In verse 13 of the same chapter Paul goes on to say that this same Holy Spirit who enables us to confess Jesus as Lord baptizes us into Christ's body, the church. Therefore it is the *faith* the Spirit inspires in us which makes us part of Christ's body, so that we can play our part in serving the others.

The church is also like a flock of sheep, very dependent on Christ their shepherd, who provides for them by appointing under-shepherds to care for them in his name. The question here is, 'How do I become a sheep?' Christ's fullest use of this picture is in John 10, and there in verse 4 he makes it clear that his 'sheep', the members of his flock, are those who have heard the voice of the shepherd (that is himself) and responded by following him.

The fourth picture was of the church as a family, of which God is Father and we the children in a community of love. How do we become God's children? In the same way as we become stones, limbs and sheep – by believing in Christ, for 'to those who believed in his name, he gave the right to become children of God' (John 1:12; cf. Galatians 3:26).

All these points enable us to give one clear answer to our question. What entitles us to membership of a church is our response of faith to the call of Christ which came to us in the preaching of the gospel. It was on these lines the apostles proceeded when they went out to obey Christ's commission. He told them in Matthew 28:19 to 'go and make disciples of all nations'. Those who became disciples by professing faith in Christ were to be baptized and taught everything else Christ had revealed or would reveal.

So when Peter preached on the day of Pentecost he called on his hearers to repent of their cruel and unjust treatment of Jesus and to accept gladly that God had raised him back to life to prove that his death had been in God's purpose so that all sins might be forgiven (Acts 2:38). Those who responded in this way were 'added to the church' so that they might there be taught everything else they needed to know, and together become a worshipping, serving, dependent and loving community (see Acts 2:41-47).

Therefore the answer to the question about eligibility is simple: one who has heard the preaching of the gospel of Christ and acknowledged him as Lord and Saviour is qualified for membership. Nothing less is sufficient. Being brought up in a Christian home; agreeing with Christianity as a creed; wanting to live a good life; being willing to do good to others; attending church services – none of these is adequate. All these features can be present apart from personal faith.

But neither is anything more required. No church has the right to ask for more. Some demand assent to a whole statement of doctrine, going far beyond the basic acknowledging of Christ's deity and saviourhood that we find in

Acts. Doctrinal bases for churches are, of course, good, but many of these doctrines are learned over a period of time after conversion and membership: they should not be a condition of coming into membership. At Pentecost the believers were immediately 'added to their number', and then 'devoted themselves to the apostles' teaching'.

To require more than the profession of personal conversion to Christ is to go from the gospel back to the law. What is necessary for membership is no more and no less than what is required for salvation. A church is a 'communion of saints' or, as we would probably put it today, 'a community of believers'. Are you a true believer? Did you become a Christian by responding to the call of Christ in the gospel? Then you are eligible and may take immediate steps to become a member of your local church. What these steps are is the subject of our next chapter. But before proceeding to that there is another issue we cannot avoid.

WHAT ABOUT BAPTISM?

This question will have arisen in the minds of some while reading the preceding pages. Because the emphasis has been placed on personal faith in Jesus as the only qualification, some will think baptism is therefore unimportant, perhaps unnecessary. To some this may come as a relief, to others as an offence. In your case it may put you in a quandary. If you were baptized on profession of your faith, you will not be unduly worried. Yet you may wonder: if I had not been baptized would I still be eligible for membership? If, however, you have not been baptized, the problem is more serious. Do I have to be baptized before I can be accepted into the church?

This is a question to which it is not possible to give a 'Yes' or 'No' answer. Not because there is no answer, but

Who is eligible to join a local church?

because evangelical churches are not agreed on the answer. It is a sad thing that churches which preach the same gospel and call for personal faith in Christ disagree on a number of issues to do with the local church. Among these is baptism. The answer to the question 'Do I have to be baptized?' will therefore depend, in your case, on the position taken by the church in which you are seeking membership. This you will have to discover, if you have not already done so, fitting in accordingly if you can conscientiously do so. My hope is that this book will be helpful to all types of evangelical church. Since each church has the right to determine its own policy on such issues as baptism, no one can write a book telling a church how it should go about receiving members or dictating whether or not they must first be baptized. What a book such as this can do, however, is to explain how this situation has come about and set forth the author's understanding of the right answer to the question 'Do I have to be baptized?'

Let us begin by summarizing the story of how baptism came to be administered in Christian churches as we find it in the New Testament. If you want a fuller account of this, then you could refer to my book, *I want to be baptized* (published by Grace Publications in 1986 and distributed by Evangelical Press, 12 Wooler Street, Darlington, Co. Durham, DL1 1RQ, England).

Baptism seems to have begun before the time of Jesus. The Jews had been dispersed into all parts of the Roman Empire and many of the people among whom they lived (whom they called 'Gentiles') became attracted to their religion. Those who seriously wished to give up their national religion and accept the God of the Jews were first circumcised to signify they now belonged to the Lord. But they were also baptized to signify they were washing away their false beliefs and evil practices.

When John the Baptist came preaching repentance in

the Judean desert he called the Jews themselves to be baptized. Their promised Messiah was about to appear and if they wished to be included in his kingdom they must wash away their own sins. Among those who responded was the Messiah himself, Jesus of Nazareth! Not because he had any evil practices to repent of but to identify himself with John's ministry and with the sinners he had come to save, both Jews and Gentiles. The voice of God which greeted him as he came out of the river made it clear he was not really the same as others, but was in fact God's only true Son.

From that time people began to follow Jesus and he used his first disciples to baptize them. Full Christian baptism did not come until after he had returned from the dead, when he sent his apostles out to make him known and to baptize those who responded, in the name of the Father, Son and Holy Spirit (Matthew 28:18-20). This they began to do on the day of Pentecost in Jerusalem, when the first conversions in the church age took place (Acts 2:37-40). The same happened in every town, city and village where Jesus was preached. So much did this become the established practice that Paul was able to speak of 'one baptism' (Ephesians 4:5), for baptism was one of the things all Christians and churches had in common.

Would that this were still the case! Unhappily it is not so. Baptism is no longer a mark of the unity of the churches but one of the chief areas of division. It is no use shutting our eyes to this, especially if we are to give an honest answer to our question. It would be lovely if we were in the position of the churches in Acts, but we are not. During the many centuries that have followed the apostles' time, differences have arisen over the matter of baptism. In giving a brief survey of these I am not confining myself to churches which preach the same gospel as the apostles, but considering all types of church in order to give a complete picture, for Christians tend to accept the form of baptism used in their denomination, even if they do not accept the way of salvation proclaimed by some churches in that denomination.

Differences over baptism among the churches may be expressed as follows:

1. *The different meanings attributed to baptism*

The *Roman Catholic Church* regards baptism as the way God's saving grace is actually imparted. The moment of baptism is therefore the moment of salvation, however young the recipient may be.

Lutheran and *Anglican* churches regard it as the way of entering the church and inheriting its benefits. Baptism is becoming a church member, however young the candidate.

Reformed churches believe that when God brings people into covenant relationship with himself through faith in Christ he includes their children. Baptism is the sign and seal that these children of believing parents are in the church, among the covenant people of God.

Baptist churches see baptism as the way in which the faith of the heart is publicly confessed by the believer and its benefits confirmed to him by Christ.

Other churches (or 'para-churches') understand baptism as a purely spiritual act performed by the Holy Spirit and not a ceremony with actual water. The Salvation Army and some independent churches would be of this persuasion.

2. *The different subjects eligible for baptism*

Roman Catholic, Lutheran, Anglican and Reformed churches all baptize infants as well as adults, assuming (at least in theory) that the children are the offspring of confessed believers or members of their church. Baptist churches baptize only those who can testify to a personal faith in Christ, so that baptism is never administered to infants, but only to those who have reached 'years of discretion'.

3. *The different modes employed for performing baptism*
Some pour or sprinkle water on the head; some immerse the entire body; others employ or at least allow any of these modes.

4. *The different places assigned to baptism in relation to church membership*
Some regard baptism as essential to membership. These include not only the Roman Catholics, Anglicans and Reformed, but groups of Baptists who confine membership to those baptized by immersion on profession of faith. Some of these would go further and restrict the Lord's Supper also to those baptized. However, there are other churches which teach that baptism is desirable before membership and communion but not absolutely essential.

Your church will almost certainly follow one of these traditions and expect you to conform to it if you wish to become a member. It is a pity we do not all take the same view and adopt the same practice of baptism, but these differences have grown up with the turbulent history of the church and we have to take them into account. We have to take people as they are, not as we would like them to be. It would be good if a sermon could be preached or a book written which would bring all to agreement. This is not going to happen and we must be realistic about it. The situation is complicated these days by the greater mobility of Christians. Many, when they move to another part of the country, will rightly look for a church which preaches the gospel they believe irrespective of whether it is in the denomination they previously belonged to. Sometimes this means they find a different approach to baptism and membership from what they have been used to.

All this has to be taken into account in giving an answer to our question. What we really need is to discover whether the New Testament gives us any principles which will help us decide what to do in a situation where there are radical differences over a matter such as baptism. In the view of this writer it does, and the answer to our question may be put in this way: you *should* be baptized but you do not *have* to be baptized in order to become a church member. This is not just a personal opinion, it has scriptural support. In the New Testament baptism is normal and therefore desirable for all potential church members; but it was not then and therefore is not now an absolute condition.

There are two parts to the last statement and both need explaining and justifying.

(i) *You should be baptized because baptism is normal and desirable*

The grounds for this are as follows:

(a) Christ gave an explicit command that those who believe in him should be baptized: 'Go and make disciples of all nations, baptising them in the name of the Father and of the Son and of the Holy Spirit' (Matthew 28:19).

(b) In every place where they preached Christ, the apostles baptized those who believed their message. See, for example, Acts 2:38-41; 8:12,36-38; 9:18; 10:47; 16:15,33; 18:8; 19:5.

(c) Baptism is a privilege and a gift. The command of Christ is not a legal rule or a matter of absolute morality, but a gracious invitation. Few refuse gifts or decline invitations, especially if they come from the sovereign! Baptism is such a royal gift and invitation.

(d) Baptism is the way of publicly acknowledging Jesus as our Saviour and ourselves as his disciples. Jesus made public confession a corollary of saving faith: 'Whoever acknowledges me before men, I will also acknowledge him before my Father in heaven. But whoever disowns me before men, I will disown him before my Father in heaven' (Matthew 10:32-33; see also Romans 10:9-10). Neither Jesus nor his apostles gave any other way of making this confession, such as going to the front of the meeting, raising the hand or signing a card – only baptism. Our faith seems incomplete without it.

(e) Baptism is a 'means of grace', that is, one of God's ways of blessing us. It does not save us but it does confirm his promise of salvation and therefore strengthens our relationship with him. The use of water is significant, indicating as it does washing from sin. Paul was invited to baptism with the words, 'Get up, be baptised and wash your sins away, calling on his name' (Acts 22:16). The same Paul may have been thinking of his baptism when he referred to 'the washing of rebirth' (Titus 3:5). Being baptized thus helps us to feel we are morally clean in God's pure eyes, and are beginning a new life.

(f) Baptism is a way of associating ourselves with other baptized Christians. In baptism we are saying that we accept not only Christ but those he has accepted. We are like Ruth going home with Naomi, saying that because their God is our God, his people are our people (Ruth 1:16). John said that 'everyone who loves the father loves his child as well' (1 John 5:1). In baptism we are committing ourselves to that love.

In view of all this, how can we refuse baptism? What arguments can we advance against it? As the Ethiopian eunuch said to Philip, 'Why shouldn't I be baptised?' (Acts 8:37). Surely, like him, we shall want to be baptized – and as soon as possible. Thus Ananias said to Paul, 'What are you waiting for? Get up, be baptised' (Acts 22:16). If we have already been baptized we shall be the more glad for reading these points. Yet at the same time we must not go too far in our enthusiasm and spoil this lovely means of grace, this happy privilege. We must therefore consider the other part of our statement.

(ii) *Baptism is not an absolute condition of church membership*

While the New Testament commands baptism to all believers and invites them to undergo it, it never goes so far as to lay it down as a condition *sine qua non*, that is, without which church fellowship is refused. There are excellent reasons for saying this.

(a) We are saved through faith in Christ alone, not through faith plus something else. Christ receives us because and only because we trust him, not because we are baptized. We are to receive each other on the same basis – purely and simply because Christ has received us (see Romans 15:7). If we require baptism before membership we are asking more of people than Christ requires.

(b) To make baptism a condition of membership is to add a ceremonial rule to a spiritual action. Making baptism a condition is to divest it of its 'grace' and make it 'law'. Instead of being undergone as a privilege and means of grace it becomes a qualification and means of admission. Faith entitles us to all the privileges of the church, beginning with baptism. To make it a condition of enjoying these privileges is to change its whole significance as a gift and blessing. It is to do what certain interlopers into the Galatian churches did. They wanted to add circumcision to faith before they would have fellowship. Paul called this a denial of the gospel of justification by faith only. He was not against circumcision. As a Jew he still valued it. He even encouraged it in others and circumcised Timothy. No one enforced it and it was a happy arrangement. But in the case of Titus they were trying to compel it and therefore Paul refused, because it was adding to the gospel. If you read Galatians you will see how heated Paul became over it, even though he found himself in a minority of one, with such eminent pillars of the church as Peter and Barnabas taking the opposite position! But who doubts he was right? To require baptism is not dissimilar. As a means of grace freely accepted it is wonderful. As a legal rule and condition it is misrepresented.

(c) Baptism is something between the believer and his God, not between him and the church. Peter calls it 'the pledge [literally 'response'] of a good conscience towards God' (1 Peter 3:21). It is a very inward and personal matter, the response to God's gracious call and offer that comes from the depths of our being. No one has a right to interfere in this. Paul teaches us not to apply compulsion to the conscience because of the danger of causing sin (Romans 14:23). Those with weak consciences are particularly vulnerable and can easily be made to feel guilty about baptism. If they come in a spirit of guilt they come with the wrong motive and miss its blessing. Consciences need gentle counselling not pressurizing or bullying with rule books thrown at them.

(d) It is an inadequate foundation for the unity of the local church. At first sight it may appear to enhance its unity. 'We are one because we are all baptized in the same way.' But this can be a façade covering underlying disagreements. New Testament unity arises from a common faith not a common view of baptism. Unity has to be in the heart not the flesh. Paul's picture of a united church is in

Who is eligible to join a local church?

Colossians 3:12-14: 'Therefore, as God's chosen people, holy and dearly loved, clothe yourselves with compassion, kindness, humility, gentleness and patience. Bear with each other and forgive whatever grievances you may have against one another. Forgive as the Lord forgave you. And over all these virtues put on love, which binds them all together in perfect unity.'

Those whose unity with each other had previously been through race, religion, ritual, culture or class (see v.11) had now found a unity of love. There can be agreement on baptism in a church without faith and love and their fruits. There can also be disagreement over baptism with faith and love. Those united in the second way have a better bond than that of baptism.

The same applies to the unity between churches. Baptism can divide churches from churches. Although they are agreed in the gospel they have had to separate over baptism. They have different names and separate buildings, so that they do not worship together or co-operate in evangelism. This is a hindrance to their credibility before the world.

(e) Insistence on baptism is opposed to the great New Testament principle of the priesthood of all believers, denied in the church for hundreds of years and revived only in the sixteenth century. Before that time Christians had to do what 'the church' (that is the clergy) said. They had no 'right of private judgment'. But the New Testament says all Christians are priests and all have the right to be fully persuaded in their own minds. No minister or church has the right to railroad Christians into baptism by the threat of withholding from them privileges which Christ died to give them, to which faith entitles them and which some have suffered to death to recover for them. Compulsory baptism revives the old authoritarian church-type from which the Reformation delivered us.

I want to be a church member

A church has authority to declare what it believes about baptism, but not to enforce it at the cost of refusing a true child of God admission to its fellowship. It is right and good that the case for baptism should be put to all believers who seek membership. Such should consider it carefully and prayerfully. But if, after this, they conscientiously cannot see it – whether because they were baptized in earlier years in another denomination or for some other reason – they should not be refused.

Much has had to be said on this one issue of whether or not baptism is necessary for membership, because it can be such a hot potato and lead to confusion and sorrow. However, let us remember that baptism is a gracious gift of God and its usefulness is not exhausted when it has led on to membership. It has only begun! We go on to live as baptized people.

> We have been baptized in the name of Jesus. Let us do everything in the name of Jesus.
>
> We have had the names of the whole Godhead pronounced over us. Let us honour God in all his persons.
>
> We have confessed faith in the Lord Jesus. Let us hold firm to our faith.
>
> We have declared our repentance from sin. Let us not return to it.
>
> We have been washed by the Spirit in the blood of Christ. Let us keep ourselves clean and pure.
>
> We are renewed, regenerate. Let us live the new life.

Every day when you wake up say: 'Thank you, Lord, I am baptized in your name. Let me live consistently with that today.'

3
WHAT IS THE PROCEDURE FOR JOINING A CHURCH?

If you have accepted the argument of the first two chapters you will now be convinced about two matters:

1. that it is right and good for you to become a member of your local church;
2. that as a true believer in Christ you are eligible.

So where do you go from here? How do you go about becoming a member? Once again we cannot turn to a passage of Scripture which will set it all out for us. But neither can we do this, for example, for marriage. The Bible says much about what marriage is but next to nothing about the procedure for entering it, the wedding ceremony and subsequent celebrations. We have to sort it out from Scripture principles and common sense.

Joining a church is not unlike marriage. In both cases two parties are coming together to be united. For you must remember that when you come into membership the existing members are not passive. They are receiving you in the same way as you are joining them. As in marriage, there has to be mutual consent openly expressed on both sides. So if there is such a thing as a procedure it applies to the existing members as well as the potential one.

We will therefore look at the matter in this way: first, your part, then that of the church you are joining.

1. *You, the believer, deliberately seek to join your local church*

When Paul left Damascus, where he had been based since becoming a disciple of Christ, he travelled to Jerusalem where he 'tried to join the disciples' (Acts 9:26). That means more than making a request to attend their meetings. Most of these were public anyway, for many were held in the Temple precincts where all and sundry gathered. What it means is that he wanted the church in Jerusalem to accept him as one of them, as a fellow believer. In this he took the initiative. Although the historic circumstances are very different, yet basically you are seeking to do something similar. It is thus for you to make the first approach.

If you turn back to Acts 5:12-13 you will find some who were doing the exact opposite of what Paul was doing. All the believers used to meet together in Solomon's Colonnade (which was part of the Temple precincts). 'Noone else dared *join them*, even though they were highly regarded by the people.' This took place just after the dramatic and awesome deaths of Ananias and Sapphira. This event plus the 'miraculous signs' the apostles were performing attracted and interested the people, who came in droves to witness these things and to listen to these men. Yet each was scared of becoming one of them in case he suffered in the way Ananias and Sapphira had done. So they did the opposite of what Paul had done – they decided deliberately not to 'join them'.

The word for 'join' is most interesting. Literally it means 'glued'. It is the forming of a bond, something close and intended to be permanent. It is used for sexual relationship in 1 Corinthians 6:16. Paul's warning against fornication is based on the argument that if you join yourself to a prostitute you are 'one with her in body' just as if you were married to her. Then he goes on to use the same term of

What is the procedure for joining?

our relationship with Christ: 'He who unites himself with [or joins] the Lord is one with him in spirit.'

This is something of an indication of how you go about joining the church. You make the decision yourself and you consciously and deliberately seek to implement it by making the approach. But before you rush off and do it, take note of two thought-processes you go through in arriving at your decision. Without these your decision may be defective, just as your original 'decision' to become a Christian would have been.

Understanding

The first of these thought-processes is *understanding*. You need to come into membership knowing clearly what you are doing. You should have a firm grasp of the principles outlined in the earlier chapters. Two things in particular should be fixed in your mind:

a. That the faith which brought you to Christ and into a relationship with God has also brought you into a relationship with other believers, particularly those with whom you regularly worship. A bond has been made between you and them like the one between you and God. You are one with them.

b. That these believers together form the most special society in the world – the church of Christ. This is the most important community there is or can be; it is above philanthropic institutions, social clubs, political parties, pressure groups, classes of people, nations, races, and even the family itself.

Think of Jesus and the occasion on which he was meeting with his disciples when his mother, brothers and sisters came and asked that he should come out to them. His reply was that his disciples were a family closer to him even than they (Matthew 12:46-50). This little group was a prototype of the church. The church is a people called by God, chosen out of the world and brought together to be his priests, his worshippers, his temple; to be his sheep, his precious flock; in fact to be the very limbs and organs of the body of his beloved Son. What other society can claim such a status? It is this you are joining, not a golf club or sewing guild. It will demand your complete allegiance, for its president is not the pastor, but your Saviour and God, Jesus Christ.

Some Christians come into membership because their friends are members, or because it is expected of them, or even because they are pressurized into it. This is not good enough. It must be your own convictions of its rightness that bring you in. You need understanding.

Willingness
The second thought-process is *willingness*. The church is a voluntary society. In this respect it stands above the human family, for none of us voluntarily choose our parents, brothers or sisters. But with the divine family we make a choice. It has to be freely and willingly made. It must be something you want to do above almost anything else. When Ruth opted to remain with her mother-in-law, Naomi, it was not just out of pity for this woman who had lost her husband and her two sons in a foreign land. It was because Naomi belonged to this special people, God's people, and she, Ruth, wanted to be one of them. 'Your people will be my people and your God my God' (Ruth 1:16). That is the spirit in which to go into church membership.

The teaching we have received about the church shows how vital it is that we fit in. Stones have to fit buildings, sheep have to match the flock, limbs have to be properly connected with joints and nerves, members of a family

What is the procedure for joining?

have to be in harmony. You will only feel you fit if you come in with heartfelt willingness.

Another illustration occasionally used of the Christian church is relevant here: that of an army. Christians are 'soldiers of Christ' and the church is a fighting force against all forms of evil, against the evil one and his army (Ephesians 6:10-17). An army is trained not just to use weapons and equipment but to move as one. The excessive discipline is all to this purpose. While the soldiers retain their individuality they have to learn in many ways to be alike, even to look and act alike.

Nowhere do we see the idea of the diversity in unity of the church more than here. We retain our particular personalities but need to fit together for the sake of the battle in which we are engaged. This was what delighted Paul about the church in Colosse – he saw its 'orderly' appearance (Colossians 2:5). The members were not all out for their own way, they were anxious to fit together to be effective. How much we Christians today need to learn this! Make sure you come into church membership *understanding* what it means and being *willing* to adapt.

2. The other members gladly welcome you

In marriage each partner is asked, 'Will you take this man . . . this woman?' Afterwards each says, 'I take you . . .' There is mutual consent. So in church membership; as you join yourself to the church, the church joins itself to you. Paul said, 'Accept one another then, just as Christ accepted you' (Romans 15:7). The act of the church in receiving has to be just as conscious and willing as that of the applicant. Their role is no more passive than yours.

If the church is to feel this willingness it must satisfy itself about your Christian standing – that you are really one of them. Otherwise you will not be one with them, you

I want to be a church member

will be a member only in name. This has always been a real danger. Even in the early church there were 'false brothers' (Galatians 2:4), and some who had already been baptized had to be refused fellowship on further enquiry (Acts 8:13,21).

If the members are to receive you willingly as a brother in Christ they will need to consider and test you. The church has the Lord's authority to do this. In Matthew 18:17 he empowered churches to dismiss serious offenders, which surely implies they had power to judge their status and receive them in the first place.

Not only has the church the *authority* to do this, it has a positive *responsibility*. It is Christ's 'body', the form in which he is seen among the people of the world. We are his disciples, his witnesses. People judge the gospel of Christ, and even Christ himself, by the behaviour of the members of his church. So it is necessary for those already in the church to make a judgment before the world does, for the world's judgment will be far more severe. In other words we have to do collectively what Jesus forbade us to do individually – to judge each other (Matthew 7:1). But we must be careful how we make these judgments. They must not come from our prejudices, our personal likes or dislikes, but from the principles laid down by Christ. If the church is properly ordered and taught, it will know how to go about this.

There is one particular part of Scripture which is almost entirely devoted to this matter: John's first letter. (It would be good to have this book open in front of you.) He wrote it to the church in Ephesus about thirty years after Paul's final contact with it (Acts 20:17-38). On this farewell visit Paul warned that false teachers would come in among them; in fact they would emerge from the church itself. When John wrote years later Paul's warning had become a reality (see 1 John 2:18-19). This was probably the cause of John's writing.

What is the procedure for joining?

John's message is 'test the spirits' (4:1) – test people who claim to have the Holy Spirit, especially if they set themselves up as teachers. But the tests he proposes are as suitable for applicants for membership as they are for teachers. John presents us with three essential marks of a Christian, and it is these your church should be looking for when it considers your application.

It is important for you to know these now, before applying, so that you can test yourself before the church does. After all, when you are preparing for an examination you study the syllabus to find out what you are going to be tested on. This is even more important. Many have thought themselves converted but have been deluded. They have proved like the non-fruit-bearing soils in Christ's parable (Mark 4). Jesus warned that many would appear before him on Judgment Day expecting a place in heaven, but he would disown them (Matthew 7:22-23). 'Examine yourselves', wrote Paul, 'to see whether you are in the faith' (2 Corinthians 13:5).

(a) The first test John proposes is that of **belief**. To be regarded as a true Christian and accepted into membership you do not have to know and accept all the doctrines of Christianity. This will take you a long time. There are, however, certain indispensable ones, all to do with Jesus Christ. There were particular reasons why John selected these, to do with the situation in Ephesus, yet they apply for all time. These truths are:

i) that Jesus is true God, the divine Son (4:15);

ii) that while still remaining true God he also became a real man (4:2);

iii) that as God and man in one person he was able to do the work of 'the Christ' or 'Messiah' (5:1);

This means that he came to earth in flesh to carry out a mission for God which was to rescue sinners and bring them back to God by bearing the punishment of death due to them. There were those in Ephesus who taught that Jesus became Son of God at his baptism, but ceased to be Son just before his death. This was why John wrote 5:6-8, where the 'water' refers to his baptism and the 'blood' to his death on the cross. He was Son of God not only at his baptism but also when he died.

So do not think that the church is going to expect you to master a long detailed confession of faith and sign it before it will receive you. It will probably have such a confession and you should lose no time in coming to grips with it. But it may take some time for you to understand it all and be convinced about it. Meanwhile you may become a member on the basis of what you believe about Christ. For these are the distinctive truths of Christianity, which separate it from other faiths and from the general moral and religious stance adopted by many people in Britain. These truths constitute the gospel itself, by which people are saved.

(b) The second test is **love**. This follows hard upon the first, for in 5:1 John goes straight from saying 'everyone who believes that Jesus is the Christ is born of God' to say 'everyone who loves the father loves his child as well'. If you are truly born of God you belong to the family of which he is Father and you will love his other children.

Love is the evidence that belief is genuine faith. Believing truths can be a mere mental exercise. You know it is true heart-faith when it issues in love. There were people in Ephesus who claimed to have a special knowledge of truth (2:9) but did not love the other believers; they despised and even hated them. This was virtually admitting they were not born of God, for one who does not love

What is the procedure for joining?

is still in a state of spiritual death (3:14-15). The evidence of life is that we 'love our brothers'. This is what convinces the world, as Jesus said in John 13:35. The world is not competent to judge our doctrine, but it can judge our relationship with each other. Where it sees Christians who cannot get on with each other, it will turn away – and rightly.

So ask yourself, do you love those who are already members of the church you are attending? This is not the same as asking if you *like* them. It is easy to make this mistake, especially when you are fairly new and do not know the others very well. You may find it hard to make friends with them and conclude they do not like you. Then you will respond by not liking them or even leaving the church. This is quite wrong. We do not have to like everyone equally. There are various human factors which determine our likes and dislikes. There are bound to be some people to whom we are drawn more than others. These will be our 'friends'. It is not wrong to have some in the church who are special friends.

However, this must not stop you *loving* the others. You may be wondering how you know if you love them, when this is not the same as liking. John answers this question in 5:2 in the words 'loving God and carrying out his commands'. It leads naturally on to our third test.

(c) This is the test of **behaviour**. True belief is proved by love, and true love is shown in behaviour. Your love for God is shown by avoiding sin and practising righteousness (2:3-5; 3:4-6). This means more than just conforming to the moral standard of society. It means taking as our model Christ the perfect man. Because of this we shall never be able to say we are without sin (1:8). At the same time we shall strive through God's grace to conquer it (5:4-5).

The greatest of Christ's righteous acts was to love sinners, and his highest command to us is to love the other believers. This is not so much a matter of how we *feel* about them as of how we *act* towards them. The love of God to us is that when we were hateful to him, when we were his enemies, when we were ungodly, and everything about us was obnoxious to him so that he was angry with us, he nevertheless *acted* kindly towards us. He did not kill us or starve us into submission, but continued to pour good things upon us (Matthew 5:45). In fact he went further and sent his Son to suffer in our place (John 3:16).

Christian love is therefore what we *do* for each other, how we behave to each other, regardless of what we feel or how we are treated. You love the other members by regarding them as true children of God like yourself, respecting them, valuing their gifts and their contribution to the life of the church, sympathizing with them in their problems, co-operating with them in their efforts. Do you want to do this? Will you start now? Sit next to different people in the meetings, not always in the same place, next to the same person, with whom you feel 'safe'. Enquire about their welfare, offer them help when needed, visit their homes and have them in yours. Above all pray for them at least once a week by name. This is how you obey the commands of God and fulfil the law of Christ.

So how do you make out in this examination? Remember that the three are all one, all interlinked, each helps and proves the others. If you lack one it means the others are defective. Then you must search your heart to see if it is really 'a new heart'. This does not mean you are expected to be perfect in all three before you can join. You must pass in all three papers, not score 100%! You must be able to respond positively and say, 'Yes, that's what I think, that's what I want to be like.' That means that at

What is the procedure for joining?

least you have the beginnings of the matter in you. The rest will follow if you keep pressing on.

But you must be acceptable to the others. Your church will have its own formal way of proceeding from here. It may have a booklet for you to read and/or a form to sign. You may have to be interviewed by a church officer, or even attend a church meeting and testify at it. These formalities vary from church to church, so you will have to enquire about the procedure and follow it. But every believer and every church should follow the principles of this chapter, for they are those of Christ himself.

4
HOW IS A NEW MEMBER RECEIVED?

Let us assume the church has said yes to your application and that all the necessary formalities are complete. What happens next? The answer is: your actual reception into membership, the moment from which you begin to be a member. When this takes place and how it is conducted will vary somewhat according to the tradition followed by the church you are joining. Some will hold the reception at a public service, at which non-members and even non-believers will be present. Others will include it in the business of their next church members' meeting, or even convene a special church meeting for the purpose.

Whatever the different arrangements one thing is almost certain – the reception will take place in the context of the Lord's Supper. Christians and churches are generally agreed that this is the most appropriate way of receiving new members. The church is the body of Christ, the flock of Jesus, and a new member or a fresh sheep is of more concern to him even than to us. Moreover it is because and only because of his death on the cross that any of us is eligible for membership in his church. Indeed it is only because of his death that there is a church at all. It is 'the church of God, which he bought with his own blood' (Acts 20:28). Paul not only wrote 'the son of God, who loved *me* and gave himself for *me*' (Galatians 2:20), but also 'Christ loved *the church* and gave himself up for *her*' (Ephesians 5:25). So the Lord's Supper, instituted in memory of his death, has a special place in the life of the church.

How is a new member received?

The Lord's Supper is a corporate act of worship, a part of the life of the church. Jesus gave it for us to observe together, not privately. Before inaugurating it he gathered his apostles together (Matthew 26:20). The first recorded occasion of their observing it was after the first conversions and baptisms had taken place and many were added to the church (Acts 2:42,46). In 1 Corinthians 10:17 Paul wrote that there is 'one loaf' of which we all partake, so that however 'many' we may be, we form 'one body'. The 'one loaf', the common bread, represents Christ as the bread of life. The 'one body' is his body, the church. In 1 Corinthians 11:18-33 he referred to their 'coming together' to 'eat the Lord's Supper'. Common food can be eaten in homes, but the Lord's Supper is for the church when it meets together.

There can be no better setting for the reception of a new member into the local church than the Lord's Supper. There we are all equal. The Lord's Supper speaks of the cross and the cross speaks of sin. We are all equally sinful, whether we have been members for fifty years or are just in the process of joining. The cross which speaks of sin also speaks of redemption. There are no degrees of redemption – we are just as much redeemed five minutes after faith as we are five years later. The cross which speaks of sin and redemption speaks of the love of God in Christ. We are all equally loved, equally precious in his sight. The Lord's Supper is an expression of our oneness in Christ. The church is to be one: one body, one flock, one family, one building. So to receive a new member, or sheep, or son or daughter, or stone, we meet at his table.

This, therefore, seems an appropriate place in our studies to give consideration to the Lord's Supper. In some churches your reception will also be your first communion. In others you may have been attending communion since your conversion. However this may be, in all probability more attendances will follow your reception than preceded it! For this reason it would be good to look into it at this point. You may already have received instruction in it. If not, it is high time you did. If you have, it will help to have it placed on permanent record for future reference.

THE LORD'S SUPPER

Our main needs as we come to the Lord's Supper are:

1. *To understand its meaning*

Have 1 Corinthians 11 open before you.

The Lord's Supper is not a meaningless ritual. All rites and ceremonies prescribed by God have a meaning. Every one of the sacrifices performed by the priests under the old covenant had something spiritual to express and teach. When the people forgot this and performed them mechanically they were reprimanded by God as being no better than pagans. The same applies to the ceremonies of the new covenant. These have been reduced by Christ from a countless number to two – baptism and the Lord's Supper. Into them the whole message and meaning of our redemption is packed.

If we perform a ceremony mindlessly we invite the Lord's rebuke. This was what happened in Corinth. They were eating and drinking 'without recognising the body of the Lord' (v.29). They were going through the motions with their minds on the meal that was to follow. So Paul tells them they were not really eating the Lord's Supper (v.20) and because they were acting like blind pagans they would be treated as such – they would bring judgment on themselves (v.29). Since they were behaving like the world they would be 'condemned with the world' (v.32). It is therefore vital we understand what we are doing and recollect this every time we come. At first it may be a living reality, but after a number of occasions it can degenerate into a mere formality.

The meaning is simple to discover because it was given us by our Lord himself when he held its prototype the night before his death. 'Do this in remembrance of me' (vv.24-25) were the words which accompanied and explained the rite. 'This is my body . . . this is my blood' said Jesus (Matthew 26:26,28). The Lord's Supper is held 'in remembrance' that the human body of our divine Lord was broken, it truly died; that the blood which had given life to that body was 'poured out' and as it did so the life flowed out of him so that he died. By the act of dying he inaugurated 'the new covenant' – the covenant predicted by Jeremiah the prophet in which sins would be forgiven, which God would 'remember . . . no more' (Jeremiah 31:34). The Lord's Supper means that those who partake with understanding are forgiven their sins because in his death Jesus bore their punishment. Paul wrote that the celebration of the Lord's Supper was a proclaiming of his death (1 Corinthians 11:26) – a rite with a meaning. Always come to it realizing this meaning.

2. *To perceive its purpose*

Why should we remember his death in this particular way? Are we likely to forget it? Do we ever forget someone dear to us who has died? Does not everything connected with our faith and our church life centre round it? Do not hymns, prayers, readings and sermons continually point to it? Of course. The fact is that a memorial is not the same as a reminder. It has other purposes, and in this case there are two:

His honour
All over the world people erect memorials – not so much to remind them of the dead as to honour them for their noble

lives or heroic deeds. Jesus chose his own memorial, the way he wanted us to give honour to his life and death. He did not want statues, carvings, pictures or plaques, but this simple re-enactment of his death. It was the way he wanted us to say 'Thank you' to him, as our monuments are a way of saying 'Thank you' to those who at great cost have done something for our countries or communities. Paul called it 'the cup of thanksgiving' (1 Corinthians 10:16). The word is 'eucharist' – a perfectly respectable word provided 'sacrifice' is not added to it!

Our blessing

He gave us the supper for our sakes as well as his own. It is a 'means of grace', a way by which God blesses us. The main blessing it brings is that of *assurance* that we really share the benefits of what he accomplished on the cross. The rite is beautifully adapted to this. We can actually feel the bread and wine in our mouths and then sinking down inside us. In just as real a way we share the benefits of his death or participate in the body and blood of Christ (1 Corinthians 10:16-17).

In this way it is similar to baptism, for both signify to us in a dramatic way how we are involved in the sufferings of Christ. Baptism takes place only once to show his work on the cross was once for all and our salvation through it is ineradicable. The Lord's Supper is performed frequently to show that the benefits which flow both from his death and our faith are continuous, and that they are the basis of our fellowship in the church.

In coming to the Lord's Table we need not only to understand what he meant in instituting it but what we are achieving by coming. These two simple but vital purposes are the things to realize.

How is a new member received?

3. To partake in the right spirit

It is important that we attend the Lord's Supper whenever it is held in our church. There are no rules in the New Testament about its frequency, nor is there a right day or time. These have been fixed by tradition. No one tradition is more correct than another. Each church has liberty to determine these matters. What is important is that when the Supper takes place all the members are there if at all possible. It is probably this consideration that should determine matters of frequency, day and time. A church should discuss this and decide on a time when the maximum number can be present. When this is does not matter. What matters is that all possible are present. The Supper is for the church, so that together it may honour Christ and receive his blessing. From the beginning of your membership, therefore, determine you will always be present except when this is not possible. If the service is at such a time as to make it impracticable, then you should make this known and seek some revision of the arrangements.

Attendance on its own, however, is not sufficient. Paul warns of the danger of participating 'in an unworthy manner' (1 Corinthians 11:27). We have to guard against this and come in the right spirit. This calls for self-examination prior to participation (v.28). The unworthiness does not refer to sin as such. We do not have to attain to sinless perfection to qualify for attendance. The Lord's death was for sinners, and his Supper is for those who know they are sinners and want his forgiveness. Unworthy participation means:

Participating without faith in Christ

We must come to the Table trusting in Christ alone, not in the fact that we are coming, nor in the church that is

I want to be a church member

meeting or the person who is leading, and not even in the ordinance itself. It is, after all, only a symbol. We are not to trust in symbols but in the one symbolized. It is not what we do at the Table that saves and helps us, but what Christ did on the cross.

Participating without understanding
The meaning and purpose of the service have been discussed earlier. It is for us to come with these simple points clearly in our minds. The minds of the Corinthians were on social and culinary matters. They were thinking of their own supper not the Lord's. Their minds were far from the suffering of Jesus on the cross and the spiritual benefits it brings. So long as they knew they were Christians it did not matter to them what was actually occupying their thoughts during the service. We must beware of this mentality. It is not enough to think, 'Yes, I am a true believer, my faith rests on Christ alone.' Our mind must be wholly occupied with our Saviour and the preciousness of our salvation. Even true believers who partake with their minds on something else, or on nothing at all, merit the Lord's reprimand. When the novelty of the occasion wears off it is easy to let the mind wander away on such things as the meal you are going to have or to a conversation you are planning with a fellow member. This is 'unworthy' participation.

Participating without love
Not only were the Corinthians failing to consider the Lord, they were failing to consider each other (vv.21,33). They were being selfish and greedy, drawing attention to their social inequalities by bringing excessive amounts of food and drink to consume at the communal meal – the *agape*, or 'love feast' – which was to follow. Some love feast! The

only love in evidence was for their own stomachs. They had no intention of sharing the contents of their hampers with the poorer members, who were thus not merely deprived but humiliated (v.22). These people were fellow believers, members of the same body and family! Paul said this was to 'despise the church of God' (v.22). They were failing to act in the spirit of Christian love and unity, which is as dishonouring to Christ as lack of faith and understanding, since Christ is in his people as much as he is in the bread and wine. 'Recognising the body of the Lord' (v.29) has two meanings, the first involves our attitude to him, the second our attitude to his followers.

Few churches these days hold a communal meal along with the Lord's Supper. This does not matter, for Christ has not commanded it. What he has commanded is that we love each other (John 13:34), a command he gave at the Last Supper. We need to examine ourselves about this in coming to the Lord's Table. It is the commonest defect in the hearts of Christians. Most come with faith and understanding, but very often there are broken relationships with other members – grudges, criticisms, jealousies. In principle this is as bad as what the Corinthians were doing. It easily happens because of the weakness of our human flesh and the subtlety of Satan. It needs a deal of self-examination and humility to get our hearts right, not only in relation to the Lord but to each other. Yet it is just as important, since the Lord's Supper is a communal act, an act of fellowship. Fellowship means love.

You and you only can attend to these things. They are inward matters. Faith, understanding and love are basically states of heart. Only you know what is happening there. The church can lay on the best Holy Communion service of all time, but it cannot prepare your heart to take part in it. So Paul emphasizes, 'A man ought to examine

I want to be a church member

himself before he eats of the bread and drinks of the cup' (v.28). Will you make this a habit each time you come to the Table?

Begin with the service which will frame your reception into membership. You, and possibly others, will have a prominent place at that gathering. The form the actual reception takes will once again depend on the particular tradition followed by your church. What will almost certainly happen is that you will be formally received with 'the right hand of fellowship'. We are not told in the New Testament to do this, but we are told that when Paul came to Jerusalem as a Christian and one that Christ was using in the conversion of Gentiles as well as Jews, he sought recognition from the other apostles. He wanted to co-operate with them, not be a rival. Their acceptance of him as a brother and fellow worker was when James, Peter, and John held out their right hand to him (Galatians 2:9). Paul took this as an indication that they 'recognised the grace given to me'.

Your acceptance into membership means just that – the church recognizing that you are in the grace of God, that Christ has welcomed you. They are obliged to welcome all whom he has welcomed (Romans 15:7). Probably words will be spoken by one or more representatives of the church. You may have the opportunity to respond. Then one or more, representing the whole membership, will extend to you his right hand, the hand which indicates power and privilege, to signify that from that moment you are one of them. You will grasp the hand with your right hand to show that you accept the fellowship they are offering you. From that moment you are fully one of them.

5
WHAT AM I COMMITTING MYSELF TO?

Romans 12 should be read in conjunction with this chapter.

No one with any sense joins an organization without first finding out what he's involving himself in. What will it cost me to join? What is the annual subscription? What are my obligations? What are the rules? What do the other members expect from me? Who are the leaders? What authority do they have over me? These are the questions anyone will ask before signing the application form.

Christians should be no less inquisitive about joining a church, although too often they tend to go blindly into it. See that you do not. You will first want the answer to the question that heads this chapter.

This is a far more important question than the one that often comes to mind at this point, namely, 'What is there in this for me?' Such a question is not consistent with the New Testament teaching about what a church is and what it is for, discussed earlier in this volume. One of the main points that emerges from seeing the church as a building, a body, a flock and a family is that it shows that each member is there not so much for his own good as for the good of the group. The state of mind that should flow from this is one that asks, 'How can I serve the other members and contribute to the good of the church as a whole?' not 'Shall I have to disturb my easy and comfortable life if I become a member? Shall I have to give up my money and my time? Shall I be tied to doing things I don't really want to do? Shall I have to give up my freedom to do as I please?'

I want to be a church member

If you have followed the spirit of the teaching summarized here you will be more like Paul who said to Jesus, 'Lord, what do you want me to do for you? I came to Damascus to kill your people, but you've shown me that what I'm doing is hurting *you*. Yet you've forgiven me for this and made me happier than ever I was before. How can I now make up for all the harm I've caused?'

It is this same Paul who in Romans 12 pleads with all Christians to have the same attitude of mind. In verse 1 he says, 'I urge you, brothers, in view of God's mercy, to offer your bodies as living sacrifices, holy and pleasing to God.' He has spent eleven chapters describing the mercy of God: how that we are sinners and rebels, yet God sent his Son not to punish but to pardon. Instead of banishing us to hell he has reinstated us in his favour. Now we are asking, 'What can we begin to do to make it up to him?'

The way Paul answers this question is interesting and fits the matter in hand like a glove. For he immediately begins to talk about the church, as you will see if you read from verse 4 onwards. He is saying: the way God wants you to say 'Thank you' for what he's done to save you in Christ is not necessarily to go out to some benighted country and preach, but to join your local church and serve the members. He may want *some* to go abroad, but he wants *all* to serve their fellow Christians in the local church.

Do you see the point? Commitment to the local church is not an 'optional extra', it's standard practice – it's on all the models. You cannot buy a car without certain standard fitments, and you cannot become a Christian without the basic commitments: serving your fellow Christians in the church. That is why 'What am I committing myself to?' is the real question. If we think on these lines we do not need to ask, 'What is there in it for me?' For if everyone is serving everyone else, we will all be served besides doing the serving. In the Christian church we do not have some, as it

What am I committing myself to?

were, sitting at the table doing all the eating while others stand behind doing all the serving. We all eat and we all serve.

Now that our basic thinking is right we can come to the practicalities and see what these commitments are. We can divide them into two kinds: those which relate to all members, and those which refer particularly to our responsibilities to the leaders.

COMMITMENTS TO ALL OUR FELLOW MEMBERS

Obviously these include the leaders, who are basically the same as other Christians and members, but have special functions to perform. All these arise out of Paul's words in Romans 12:5: 'each member *belongs* to all the others'. This is how we need to see the church. It is not like a supermarket where a number of people find themselves in the same place at the same time for the same purpose, but have no other connection with each other. In a church we 'belong' to each other. If this is so, it explains the commitments.

1. *Meeting together*

In verse 4 Paul describes the church as 'one body with many members'. The church, remember, is like a body: it has many parts, but these are of no use unless they are joined in a body. We could say the same of a machine. It has many parts, but they are useless unless they are assembled together. A factory not only has a unit which makes the parts, but another which it calls 'the assembly shop', where they are all put together. Only then does the machine work. In the same way a church is effective only when its members assemble together.

Of course, this does not mean we have to be together all

I want to be a church member

the time and live together. That has been tried many times, but it always fails because it conflicts with other divine institutions like the family. What it does mean is that when the church holds meetings the members will be there unless circumstances prevent them. It also means that even when they are not physically meeting they will be together in spirit by their thoughts, feelings and prayers for each other.

In Hebrews 10:24-25 we can see the reason for this commitment to assemble. It is only then that we can 'encourage' each other. This is one way of serving each other and we cannot perform it unless we come together. It invariably happens that Christians who neglect meeting together become discouraged and apathetic. This affects the others, for nothing is more depressing for a church than to look round and perceive absentees from its gatherings.

So here is your first commitment on joining the church. You will find out when it meets and you will be there if you possibly can.

2. *Loving each other*

Just to be present at meetings is not enough. We must meet in the right spirit, and that is love. We must not sit there thinking, 'Aren't I good to be at church today?' Our thoughts should be on the others. Jesus said this is how the world will recognize who the Christians are – by their love for each other: John 13:34-35. Paul writes on similar lines here in verses 9-10.

But what does it mean to 'love one another'? Paul spells that out too. It is all to do with our being a body, where the parts are linked not just by visible joints but by a common nervous system, which is virtually invisible yet very real. In terms of church membership this means:

What am I committing myself to?

Sharing

We feel what others feel; we share in their joy or sorrow (v.15). We do this by enquiring of each other's welfare, listening to each other, then responding either with joy or sadness. Paul says this is just how the body behaves (1 Corinthians 12:25-26).

Bearing

We do this when we find someone's sorrow or difficulty is too great just to talk about or listen to. We actually take it upon us and help them to bear it. We get them to realize they are not alone in their grief or pain, but we are *feeling* it with *them*, which is what 'sympathy' means. You do not respond to complaints and tears by back-slapping and exhortations to 'cheer up' (Proverbs 25:20), but with your own tears (v.15).

Caring

Loving is not all talking and feeling, it may require action. Verse 13 means that we have to share our time, effort, money, or home during the period of affliction. Love can be very demanding, but it is one of our most vital commitments.

3. Serving each other

Look at verses 6-8. Each part of our physical body has a function to perform, and is made in such a way as to be able to perform that function. So it is in the church. Look at verse 4: each of us has some ability by which we can contribute to the well-being of the church (1 Peter 4:10). The very diversity of the gifts therefore helps the unity. For a church to be entirely composed of speakers would be just as monstrous as if a body were all mouth.

Romans 12 goes on to list the gifts (vv.6-8), as does 1 Corinthians 12:7-10, 14-20. However, we must remember that these are only examples, not complete lists. Also they relate to the condition of the churches at that time. They are not to be applied in a rigorous way today. Some of them may no longer be relevant, while there may be fresh ones to meet the needs of today's church. The churches in Rome and Corinth did not need car drivers and tape recorder operators, but these are very useful contributions to today's churches. On the other hand they needed such as prophets and healers who were prominent in a way quite inappropriate now.

We have to be sensible and humble about these things, as Paul says in verse 3. Mainly we must learn the purposes of these gifts and abilities. Why are we given them? In general, to serve and help each other, and thus improve the quality of our church life. In particular:

(a) *to edify or build each other up*
In 1 Thessalonians 5:11 Paul tells us to 'encourage one another and build each other up'. In Ephesians 4:12 he says that Christ has given gifts to his church to enable the members to do just this – 'that the body of Christ may be built up'. In 1 Corinthians 12:7 he says that the Spirit distributes gifts among the members 'for the common good'. There are 'different kinds of service' (v.5) to be performed and the Spirit sees there are people in the church able to perform them. So when you join a church you are committing yourself to one of the 'kinds of service'. You are not there just to receive help but also to give it. You will need to find out what you can do and what God wants you to do.

But you must be sure you do it for the good of the whole body, not for yourself. Some Christians fancy themselves as singers. Some even go so far as to join a particular church because it has a choir or group they want to be involved in. Their thoughts are on exercising their gift or even showing it off, not on how they can help the general good. Don't be like this. Purify your motives. Don't put the cart before the horse. The question is not, 'What gift can I display to the people?' but 'How can I help the people?'

(b) *to correct those in error*

A Christian may succumb to the weakness of the flesh, the lure of the world or the wiles of the devil. He may fall morally or doctrinally. It is the duty of those still standing on their feet to pick up the fallen brother (Galatians 6:1). Although leaders have a particular part to play here, the New Testament lays it squarely on the shoulders of all members as in Hebrews 12:15-16. The word here translated 'see' is interesting, because it is the word from which we get 'overseer' or 'bishop', the term which describes the elders or pastors of the church. The apostle is saying that when a Christian is falling away we should all act as pastors to him. If possible we should not wait until he has actually fallen, but try to spot the danger and head it off. This is what he means by seeing to it that 'no bitter root grows up' – do not wait for the fruit, nip it in the bud, stop it at its roots.

Of course, we have to do all this in the right spirit: 'restore him gently. But watch yourself, or you also may be tempted' (Galatians 6:1). Do not be censorious, do not gloat, do not be offended in a self-righteous way. Realize that but for the grace of God you might be in that position. Remember the occasion when the Jews brought to Jesus a woman whom they had caught committing adultery (John 8). Christ was more severe with the accusers than the accused! He knew she had been set up. So he attacked *their* consciences. No one who is unaware of his own weakness or proneness to error has the right to charge another with sin.

Put your spirit right and be ready if necessary to warn a fellow Christian of danger, or to lift him up if he falls.

4. Keeping the peace

Look at Romans 12:18; also Ephesians 4:3 and Hebrews 12:14. The church is a body and order is as essential to it as to a human body. How much discomfort and pain we suffer when there is quarrelling between one or more parts of our body and the rest of it! The sad thing is that in the church it is possible to be performing the other commitments and yet doing much damage. This was happening in Corinth. They were certainly assembling together and using their gifts and abilities. But they were acting in a competitive and partisan spirit and so causing division. Their meetings were doing 'more harm than good' (1 Corinthians 11:17). They were divided against each other. There was no peace.

When we join a church we undertake to do all possible to maintain the peace. To fulfil this commitment we have to cultivate certain attitudes of mind. We shall only behave rightly to each other if we think and feel rightly about each other. So when Paul writes about peace and unity in Romans 12 and in Ephesians 4 he dwells on certain attitudes.

Tolerance

We are to bear with each other (Ephesians 4:2). We are to put up with their foibles and erratic behaviour. Of course he is not referring to moral lapses or doctrinal aberrations. We are to 'correct' these, as we saw in the last point. He refers to those more trivial situations, where things get blown up out of all proportion. We can say that in most churches division over doctrine and morals is rare. It is usually due to clash of personality, petty foibles and the desire for one's own way in the manner in which certain activities are conducted.

Paul tells us how to react when people get angry or awkward, when they criticize or even abuse us. We do not react or reply in kind (Romans 12:14,17). We keep our cool, we practise self-control. Usually this will take the heat out of the situation and peace will be restored. Our difficult brother may be convicted by our example and learn to control himself in future. Most things which divide churches are not worth all the bother they cause. We must get things in perspective: peace, order and unity are far more important than most of the things which divide.

Humility

In Romans 12:16 Paul tells us that the way to live in harmony is to be humble about ourselves. Do not think too highly of yourself (v.3). Do not think you are always right and that the others must always give way and come to your position. Try to think dispassionately about the other person's point of view. Value him and his suggestions (Philippians 2:3-4). Do not be offended by his criticisms; he may be right and you wrong. Do not join the church with the idea that you are going to reform it and put everyone right. Come in the spirit of willingness to learn from others.

Striving for a common mind

This is the meaning of the first sentence of Romans 12:16: 'Live in harmony with one another', that is, having the same outlook. With tolerance and humility it is possible for Christians to come to see things in the same way. A few hints as to how to achieve this may be helpful.

a) Dwell more on the things you have in common than on those on which you may differ. In Ephesians 4, when appealing for peace and unity, Paul outlines the main truths of the faith in verses 4-6. These are the important things and on these we agree. Dwell more on these than on things on which you might disagree.

b) Do not fight against each other but join together to fight the common enemy (Philippians 1:27-28). Our real enemies are outside the church: sin, the world, untruth, the devil. Get together and fight these. Do not aid their cause by fighting each other. Evangelical Christians are good at shooting themselves in the foot and scoring own goals. No wonder the world laughs and passes by.

c) Make your relationship with Christ your main priority. This is the basis of his appeal for peace in Philippians 2:1-2 – the supreme desire to please Christ and glorify him by resembling him. If we put this first rather than our own way, we shall have peace and unity in our church. But not automatically! We have to work at it. We have to make every effort to bring it about (Ephesians 4:3). Then when we have it let us redouble our efforts to keep it! It is no use hiding the fact that joining a church is taking on a hard job. But it is best to go into it with your eyes open and know what you are taking on. Nor is that all!

COMMITMENT TO THE LEADERS

We shall be looking more closely at leadership later. Just for the present accept the idea that your church has leaders and that this is right. After all, in the human body some of the functions are controlling ones, especially the mind, the brain and the eye. Similarly in the church there are members who are charged with leading and teaching, as you can see in Romans 12:6-8. Members have special commitments to them.

What am I committing myself to?

1. *To appoint them*

Every group of people has to have its leaders, from the local football club to the state. We cannot do everything by majority vote; a smaller number must be given power to make decisions on behalf of all. Also, all our New Testament analogies include leadership: a building has an architect; a body has a head; a flock, a shepherd; a family a father. The church's head of course is Christ, but since he is not with us bodily he has appointed 'pastors and teachers' to lead in his name (Ephesians 4:8-11). They are particularly entrusted with teaching his Word, because this is the best way of ensuring that he keeps his own headship over the church.

It is clear that not all members of the church lead it or teach it. But they all have a place in saying who does lead it. The original apostles were appointed directly and personally by Christ himself. But when they went out into the world preaching the gospel and forming the believers into churches, they involved the people in choosing who their leaders would be. Later we shall look at the way in which this was done. At this point it is enough for you to realize this is one of your commitments. At some stage in your church life you will probably be involved in the appointment of deacons or elders.

2. *To submit to their leadership*

When the New Testament speaks to church members about their relationship to their leaders it uses words like 'esteem', 'honour', 'obey' and 'submit'. It wants us to recognize the authority given to them. This is chiefly because they are appointed by the Head of the church to govern in his place, they are 'over you in the Lord' (1 Thessalonians 5:12). Submitting to them is part of submitting to Christ.

Also, this is the only way a church can function efficiently.

A body only works when the parts obey the directions of the brain. If they do not we say it is 'spastic', with all the problems that go with that condition. It is the same in a family, an orchestra or any organization. This is the only way to make it work. So Christ does not ask us to submit to the leaders because they are special people, but 'because of their work' (1 Thessalonians 5:13). This 'work' is for the good of us all. Leaders 'keep watch over you' (Hebrews 13:17). They guard us from what will harm us. It is in our own interest to submit.

The New Testament also shows us the way to submit. Submission does not mean grovelling, being yes-men, calling them 'sir', adulating them. We treat them personally just as we do each other, even using their first names. But recognizing their particular work as teachers and pastors we submit:

(a) *by accepting their teaching as from Christ*

When they take office they commit themselves to being servants of the word of Christ. We who appoint them commit ourselves to receiving that word as from Christ. So when they teach doctrine we believe it; when they give a word of encouragement we receive it warmly; when they rebuke or warn we take it to heart humbly – we do not 'shoot the messenger'; and when they exhort us to duty we carry out their instructions.

(b) *by following their lead*

They 'direct the affairs of the church' (1 Timothy 5:17). They ponder, pray, research and consult before coming to the church with their decision. Although they are not infallible, their decisions will usually be the best and the members should go along with them. Even if members do not agree with them all, it is better to concur for the sake of the church's unity. Members of an orchestra may not agree 100% with the conductor's interpretation of a piece of music, but it is better to go along with it than to play at their own tempo and produce cacophony.

3. *To support them financially*

The Scriptures tell Christians to give of their substance and to take up collections. These funds are administered by the leaders for a variety of purposes:

(a) *to support themselves and their families*
Some leaders will give up their secular employment in order to teach the Word of God and take care of the church. This makes them dependent on those to whom they minister. Those who appoint them thus have an obligation to provide for them (Galatians 6:6).

(b) *to enable them to do the work to which they are called*
Life in the time of the apostles was relatively simple, but they required horses and mules and passages on ships, for which the help of the churches was needed. Life is more complex today. To do the work of the ministry requires houses, cars, public transport, phones, stamps, books, word processors, printing, etc. In addition to their living expenses, leaders need funds for these other purposes.

(c) *to care for the needy among them*
The collections taken by Paul from the churches were all for this purpose – to meet the material needs of Christians in other places where there was famine or some other disaster. Although poverty among us is far less, there will still be some in need, either in the local church or in other places. This is to be supplied not from the pockets of the leaders but from the common fund.

(d) *to provide and maintain a meeting place*
The early Christians often hired public halls in which to meet, and for these they would have to pay a rent. We often have the luxury of our own buildings, and these have to be maintained. The leaders are responsible for seeing to this, and the members for providing the funds necessary.

It is obviously a very important commitment on joining a church that you give for its work out of your income, whether this be a wage, an allowance, a pension or other benefit, or even pocket money. The New Testament does not lay down an amount you should give, which is why churches do not fix a membership fee or annual subscription as other organizations do. What it teaches is that we should give in proportion to what we receive. You will need to read carefully through 2 Corinthians, chapters 8-9, to get the main principles of Christian giving. You will find the stress falls on willingness rather than amount. We are to give thankfully (9:5), cheerfully (9:7), trusting in God (9:8-11) and in a spirit of sharing (8:13-15). We are to look not at what other people give but how Christ gave himself (8:9). If our spirits are right we shall give generously and the church's needs will be met.

4. To co-operate with them in their work
The leaders are not there to do all the work, only to lead the members in sharing the work together. They are appointed to train us to minister to each other (Ephesians 4:12) and to go out witnessing in the world. As already seen, they do not do all the pastoring; we are all responsible for each other; we are our brother's keeper. But we need help, instruction and training to do it. In the same way, it is not for the leaders to pull the crowds in and lead souls to Christ. They are there to help us do this. We all do the work together. It is a combined effort.

6
WHO LEADS THE CHURCH?

Now that you know you have commitments to your church's leaders, you will want to know about these leaders. If you have been involving yourself in the life of your local church you will already have come to realize that certain of the members are more prominent than others. There are, out of the many, just a few who take on the main duties: leading services, preaching the word, giving out notices, playing the accompaniment, taking the collection and giving out hymn-books. If you attend weekday meetings or special groups you may find others presiding or taking leading roles.

If your church is very small you may find that just one person leads the worship and preaches; one person gives out notices; and possibly the same one who gives out the books also takes the collection. But in all churches you will find some form of leadership. If you are really anxious to know what Scripture says about the church, you will want to see where all this comes in the New Testament. To whom exactly are you 'committed' in the way described in the previous chapter? Just the preacher? or the organist as well? The secretary? or the steward also?

Let us take a look at what we find in the Bible about 'leadership in the church'.

1. *The One 'Leader'*
Read Ephesians 1:18-22

Strictly speaking you will never find the noun 'leader' used of any of the people just mentioned. You will find the expression 'those who lead' (although the NIV translates this phrase as 'leaders': Hebrews 13:7,17,24). But the noun 'leader' in the original language is reserved for one person – Jesus Christ. He is the only one appointed to be 'head' of the church, and that by God himself (Ephesians 1:22).

This is why his leadership of God's people is foretold and foreshadowed in the Old Testament – because it makes his appointment truly official. In any walk of life how do we know who are the true leaders? Anyone can stand up and say, 'I'm in charge here.' But the true leader is the one whose office has been announced beforehand by the competent authority.

Therefore Jesus' headship of the church did not await his appearance on earth or his return to heaven. We find him leading the people of Israel – for example in Joshua's time as 'commander of the army of the Lord' (Joshua 5:14). We find several other statements about his authority: Isaiah 55:4; Micah 5:2,4; Psalm 118:22. This last is the one quoted in Ephesians 2:20. So Paul is on firm biblical ground when he asserts that 'God placed all things under his feet and appointed him to be head over everything for the church' (Ephesians 1:22).

This same passage tells us that, although he was appointed long before his appearance in the world and was in fact exercising his headship, he did not fully enter on his office until he had completed his redeeming work and brought his church from all nations into being. The Old Testament's headship was just a preliminary to this greater headship. It was when God 'seated him at his right hand in the heavenly realms' that he 'appointed him to be head over everything for the church'.

For it was *as man* and *for man* that he is made head. He became a man to represent us in his unrepeatable sacrifice on the cross, to suffer sin's punishment in our place. Then he rose – still as man – and ascended back to heaven

Who leads the church?

in order to work out the fruits of his conquest of sin, death, and the devil. The power he received in order to do this was total and universal – 'head over everything'. This is essential. He must have this power in order to bring to God everyone his Father gave him (see John 17:2). Having brought them in he must have power to keep them safe – power over those who would harm them, both in the natural and the supernatural world. This is the power God has given him (Ephesians 1:21).

He will go on exercising this power until the time comes for him to return as Judge. Paul uses similar words to those of Ephesians 1:22, when he says in 1 Corinthians 15:25, 'He must reign until he has put all his enemies under his feet'. 'Then the end will come' and he will hand the kingdom back to the Father on whose behalf he has been ruling it (v.24).

It is necessary to be clear about all this because we tend to get our concept of leadership from the world. Jesus warned us against this in Luke 22:24-27. The greatness and authority possessed by kings belong only to one person in the church – Christ. The one we are really committed to is Christ himself. The rest of us, whatever our office, are servants. Leaders in the church are really servants of the people and servants of Christ, and we must neither fear them on the one hand nor idolize them on the other. They are not 'heads' and must never be referred to or thought of as such. But that does not mean they have no place in the government of the church, as we must now see.

2. *The deputy leaders*

Although the Lord Jesus is the only Head and Leader of the whole church and of every particular church, he does not rule directly. He does not physically come to our meetings, 'take the chair', or preach the sermon. Nor does he write our basis of membership for us or make the day-to-day decisions. He appoints others to do these things in his name.

The first ones he chose were the apostles. During his life on earth Jesus selected twelve men to go about with him hearing what he said and watching what he did. He was trying to bring them to see for themselves that he was the promised Messiah, the divine Saviour. As soon as they saw that and openly expressed it, he went on to bestow his authority on them. Read Matthew 16:13-19 again. In that last verse he made them his deputies to rule the church: 'I will give you the keys of the kingdom of heaven.' Keys are symbols of authority and power; the key opens and shuts, admits or excludes.

The apostles were entrusted with a particular and unique authority – to define the new truth Jesus had come to reveal, to complete the Word of God by adding the 'New' to the 'Old' Testament. The books of the New Testament were written by the apostles and their colleagues, and they tell us what Christ said and did, what God meant by these things, what we learn from them and what we have to do about them. We call this 'doctrine and ethics'. Christian 'doctrine and ethics' are defined in the New Testament.

When the apostles died they were not replaced. Neither they, nor Christ, nor the churches appointed men with this power. The Bible was complete and there was no need for further apostles. Nor was there need for men with authority over the whole church. Instead men were appointed in each church to govern in Christ's stead. They were to do this by declaring in the churches the words of the apostles, that is, by preaching the Word. But although their authority was to be less than that of the apostles (since they brought no fresh revelation and were limited to a local church) they were still Christ's deputies. So we find words used of him are used of them. As Jesus is called

Who leads the church?

'overseer' (1 Peter 2:25), so they are 'overseers' (5:2). As Jesus is 'chief shepherd' (5:4), so they are 'shepherds' (5:2). As Jesus is 'over' the whole church (Ephesians 1:22), so they are 'over' their particular churches (1 Thessalonians 5:12). These local leaders are just as much given by Christ as were the apostles. 'When he ascended on high, he . . . gave some to be apostles . . . some to be pastors and teachers' (Ephesians 4:8-11). They are 'over' the churches but 'under' Christ, and their duty is to proclaim and apply the word he gave to the apostles.

These men are given various names. The main ones are elders, overseers, pastors and teachers. They are also called 'those who lead' or 'those who are over' the churches. For the sake of simplicity we will mainly use the term 'elder'. For whereas all the other terms describe their functions, this one refers to their actual office or title.

Eldership was not invented only when the first New Testament churches were planted. It is an ancient institution and is secular as well as religious. The ancient Egyptians had elders (Genesis 50:7). So did the Israelites while they were in Egypt (Exodus 3:16-18). When Moses became leader of this nation he appointed seventy elders to assist him in explaining God's law, legislating, and adjudicating among the people (Exodus 18:13-24). After they settled in their land there were elders of tribes (Deuteronomy 5:23) and of cities (19:12).

No doubt when Israel became ruled first by 'judges' and then by kings the elders lost some of their powers. However, after they had spent seventy years away in Babylon in exile, they had no king, and local elders again became important. Also, the system of synagogues in each town developed, and these were ruled by elders (Luke 13:14).

So it happened that when the apostles came to plant churches in these towns they would find people in positions of leadership who could be used in the churches.

Where there were Jewish communities, the believing synagogue elders became church elders – for example, in Corinth (Acts 18:8,17). Where the converts were mostly Gentiles, those already prominent in the community were obvious candidates for eldership, as for example Tyrannus in Ephesus (Acts 19:9).

It was the policy of the apostles to appoint elders as soon as possible after forming a church. Paul did this in the Galatian churches before he left the area (Acts 14:23). In other places he left one of his colleagues behind to set up an eldership: Luke in Philippi,* Timothy in Ephesus (1 Timothy 1:3; 2 Timothy 2:2) and Titus in Crete (Titus 1:5). These men were to be regarded by the churches as called by the Holy Spirit (Acts 20:28).

But what would happen when there were no apostles left? or even prophets or evangelists like Luke, Timothy and Titus? Who was to make the appointments then? Were synagogues or community elders automatically made church elders? What if there were too many? or none at all?

Actually the problem is not so difficult. From the very beginning the apostles involved the Christians in appointments to office in the church. The first officers were men required to assist the apostles in the very earliest days of the church in Jerusalem. In Acts 6:3 the Christians were told to 'choose seven men' to whom the apostles could delegate responsibility. The apostles simply laid down the guiding principles, the Christians chose the actual men. Then in the Galatian churches, where the text says the apostles 'appointed elders' (Acts 14:23), the word means 'by stretching out the hand', a probable reference to voting.

---

* This conclusion is drawn from the fact that Luke writes in the first person (we) in Acts 16, and the third person (they) in Acts 17. The inference is that he remained in Philippi.

This is why the NIV margin reads 'had elders elected' – that is, by the people.

What was needed as the apostles died out was information about the qualities to look for in potential elders. The apostles possessed a supernatural gift of discernment, but this did not mean they had a magic touch which required no thought. They still worked on principles, as Acts 6 shows, and these they eventually committed to writing in those letters written to the colleagues who had been left to see to this matter in certain churches – Timothy in Ephesus and Titus in Crete. These are the principles for us to apply in our churches today. Those leading must be men of this kind. If we conflate 1 Timothy 3 with Titus 1, we find the main qualities required of elders. It would help if you had your Bible open at these two passages.

THE APPOINTMENT OF ELDERS

This is based on the qualities that are seen in their lives.

1. *A heart for the work*

In 1 Timothy 3:1 we read, 'If anyone sets his heart on being an overseer, he desires a noble task.' If a man's heart is not in the job he will be unhappy and therefore unable to do the job well. It is not wrong to want to be an elder, but the desire must be for the right reason – for the 'task' itself, not the name, the office, the position, the power, or the money (!).

What is this 'task'? It is:

(a) to *serve* the people (Romans 12:7) – that is, to meet their needs, not to give them orders, as secular leaders do (see Luke 22:24-27);

(b) to *shepherd* them, by getting them to do what shepherds do for their sheep – to feed themselves. The elder is a 'pastor', who feeds the sheep by expounding to them the Word of God (Acts 20:20-21,27-28,32). At the same time he has to keep them away from food which may seem nice but is actually poisonous. That is, he has to smell out false teaching and warn them against it (Titus 1:10-11). Otherwise, they will become food for wolves, for the enemies of the gospel (Acts 20:29-31). To carry out all this, like a shepherd he has to 'round them up', keep them together, prevent them from wandering away from the flock. He has to be a watchman (Hebrews 13:17).

So the work is not so glamorous as might appear from outside. It is not just preaching high-sounding sermons; there is much hard work behind the scenes. The elder must have a 'heart' for all this too, not for the sound of his own voice.

2. *The ability for the work*

The Bible refers to elders as able or gifted men (Exodus 18:21). The gifts and abilities lie in two areas:

Teaching

An elder must be 'able to teach' (1 Timothy 3:2; 2 Timothy 2:2,24; Titus 1:9). A good teacher of the Word of God is one who has first of all a good grasp of the gospel in his own mind and is very clear on the issues. He has deep convictions about its truth and necessity. He can give lucid instruction and make others as clear about the gospel as he is himself. Also by forceful encouragement he makes them as convinced as himself; he can elicit a response from both believers and unbelievers. Moreover he will have the wisdom to see how the principles apply to particular situations in his church and in the lives of individuals. This may sound a tall order, but we must remember that in New Testament churches there were several elders, some of whom would have abilities in one direction, others in another.

Supervising

An elder is an 'overseer' and must have managerial gifts so that he can keep the affairs of the church in order and weld the people into a family. This is why he first has to prove himself as a husband and father (1 Timothy 3:4; Titus 1:6). He has to be not so lenient that things get out of hand, but not so overbearing that the people feel bullied. He must combine the gentleness of the nursing mother with the firmness of the father (1 Thessalonians 2:7-12). Both these tasks are considered more fully later in the chapter.

3. *The character for the work*

Without the right character, no amount of zeal or ability will fit a man for the work of an elder. The apostle's instructions focus on four traits of character.

Moral

He must be 'above reproach' (1 Timothy 3:2). This does not mean someone who never sins, but rather one whose life does not contradict his message. He preaches repentance, a changed life, holiness, love for Christ and so on; and his own life should illustrate these truths. The verses in 1 Timothy 3 and Titus 1 give some details, especially about his marriage, which should be a good one. He is expected to be a good example both to the Christians under his care and to the world outside.

Mature

He must be mature, both as a man and a Christian. The very word 'elder' denotes a certain seniority, and the passages under review suggest he is someone who has grappled with temptations and problems and come out on top. This will make him a person who can withstand emotional pressure, is not too sensitive to criticism or bad feelings, and is not easily offended. In 1 Timothy 3:6 Paul refers to his spiritual maturity, particularly the cultivation of humility and freedom from jealousy – the trap into which Satan fell and into which he seeks to lead others.

Self-disciplined (1 Timothy 3:2-3; Titus 1:7-8)

He must be someone who has himself well under control – his appetites, his temper, his tongue, his ambition, his financial interests. He should be diligent and hard-working, able to organize his time, so that a due proportion is given to secular work (if any), to church work, to the family and to leisure.

Generous and hospitable (1 Timothy 3:2; Titus 1:8)

The work of an elder is chiefly concerned with people. He spends time with them – sometimes with the whole church, sometimes with individual members. He is always having to give out, and must therefore be happy to share his time, his thoughts, his emotions, and if necessary his home and earthly goods (see Acts 20:35).

All this will help you to see why our churches have so few elders! It will also help you to respect and esteem those who have been found suitable for the work, for they are rare men indeed. One day you may be called on to share in the appointment of an elder. This is why you need to know what qualities to look for.

THE RESPONSIBILITIES OF ELDERS

This is where we will see more clearly why such a high standard is set for those to be appointed elders. It is for a very practical reason – the nature of the work they have to do. We can look at this under two heads.

1. *Supervising*

The elder is called an 'overseer' (1 Timothy 3:1), one who is 'over' the people of God in a local church (1 Thessalonians 5:12), or who leads them (Hebrews 13:7,17,24).

It is important that we do not take our ideas of this supervising work from the world and conjure up pictures of tyrannical dictators, bullying foremen and authoritarian schoolmasters. In the church supervising is essentially ministerial – it is serving, not dominating. Of this Paul himself was the supreme example, as he said to the elders of Ephesus in his farewell meeting with them (Acts 20:18-19).

All the duties connected with supervising are ministerial. There is *caring* – the elder must 'take care' of the church as a father does his family (1 Thessalonians 2:7, 11), which indicates total care. There is also *protecting*. The elder is a shepherd, part of whose task is to protect feeble, vulnerable sheep from wolves (Acts 20:28-31). In the New Testament 'wolves' means false teachers who try to lure Christians from Christ. The elder has to discern these, oppose them and warn his people (Titus 1:10-16).

Supervising also involves *keeping order*. The church is God's family and should behave like a family: the people must know how they ought 'to conduct themselves in God's household, which is the church of the living God' (1 Timothy 3:15). This does not mean they must speak in hushed whispers in a religious building. It refers to how they should behave towards each other, that is, like members of a family. This is why it is a good thing for an elder to have had experience in managing a family (vv.4-5). It will help him to encourage people to relate rightly to each other, to organize the affairs of the church as he does those of his home, and if necessary to discipline those who misbehave or are slack, as he does his own children. This is all part of his work as elder (Titus 1:13, 2:15, 3:10).

Supervising also means *personal counselling*. It will not be enough to make general statements from the pulpit. He will need to explain them in more detail to those who do not understand them and to answer their questions. He may be called upon to advise them on personal or family problems. He will have to encourage those who do not respond to the preaching by exhorting and urging them privately. He may have to warn some who show indifference or even opposition to the word he preaches. Paul did this (Acts 20:31) and instructed other elders to do likewise (v.28). The elder is like a watchman (Hebrews 13:17) who sees the danger signals and moves into action before the enemy does.

Nor is it just by his words he does all this. His life is to be a light which people will follow. Paul was so careful about the way he lived that he could tell people to follow him (1 Corinthians 11:1)! Moreover he taught that all elders should be able to say this (1 Timothy 4:12).

How thankful you should be if your church is one to which Christ has given elders to help you in all these ways! How careful you should be to follow their lead and benefit from their ministry! But there is more:

2. Teaching

Elders are called to teach the Word of God to the congregation (Romans 12:7; Ephesians 4:11). They are pastors, shepherds, whose main job is to see that the sheep feed well. The elder has to lead Christians to 'green pastures' by setting before them the 'whole will of God' from his Word, as did Paul (Acts 20:27).

There are several aspects to this work of teaching. The basic idea is *instruction*, that is, explaining the Scriptures: their doctrines (what they teach about God, Christ, salvation, etc.); their ethics (what God requires of us by way of behaviour). But he has not finished when he has explained a passage or a truth simply and clearly. He then *exhorts* or encourages the people to receive and respond to the instruction – that is, to believe it, to see it in all its glory, to go forth and obey it (2 Timothy 4:2; Titus 1:9). 'Preaching and teaching' (1 Timothy 5:17) is not just lecturing or commenting. There is warmth and fervour, there is live application to the personal situations of the people present.

Then there is the negative side, which is *refutation*. Truth has to be compared with error. The elder has to be aware of wrong ideas which people may already hold, or which are abroad and may come to their ears. These he must expose, demonstrating their wrongness (1 Timothy 1:3-4; Titus 1:9-14). He must be like a shepherd who makes sure his sheep do not wander into a field of clover. For, although they might enjoy it at the time, the after-effects will be painful and may prove lethal.

But when he has done all this, perhaps the main part of his teaching ministry still lies ahead of him. His chief though most difficult task is to *train* the Christians under his care. In Ephesians 4:12 Paul said that Christ gave pastors to 'prepare God's people for works of service' – that is, to equip or train them for action. The good schoolteacher does not only talk to the pupils, he gives them 'exercises' so that they may practise carrying out the theory.

Too much ministry in our churches is theoretical. Too many Christians are content with sitting in church and listening. The whole purpose is to get them to *do* what the Word says. They need to be trained to look after themselves, to feed themselves daily on the Word so that they 'grow in grace'. They need to be trained to lead their families and teach their children (Ephesians 6:4), who are the responsibility of the parents not the pastors. They need to be trained to minister to each other and not leave all this to the elders, for a church only grows strong when Christians build each other up (Ephesians 4:12-16). They need to be trained to witness in the world, to learn how to speak to non-Christians so as to win them to the faith (Matthew 5:14; Philippians 2:16).

If you want to be a church member you will have to do more than keep awake during the sermon! You will have to be prepared to be trained to put the principles into practice: in your own life, in the church, and in the community in which you live.

Since the last apostles died there have been very few men who have had all the gifts and abilities necessary to perform these many and varied tasks of ministry in the local church. This is why the New Testament always speaks of leadership in terms of a team rather than of a single individual. The duties can then be shared around the members of the team according to the particular gifts with which God has endowed them. Because the apostles were still present during the period in which the New Testament was being composed, we do not have much material on this aspect. We find Peter encouraging it in 1 Peter 4:10-11 and Paul in Romans 12:3-8, although it is of course possible they are thinking of the whole church rather than just the eldership.

However, Paul in 1 Timothy 5:17 is clearly referring to the elders of the church. He indicates that while all elders 'direct the affairs of the church' in general, some specialize in 'preaching and teaching'. This is a demanding and time-consuming work. The apostles were directly inspired by the Holy Spirit in their public preaching and teaching. It did not involve extensive study of books and documents nor the labour of arranging their conclusions in an interesting and edifying way to the extent required since their time. They left us the record not only of their preaching (in the book of Acts) but also of their teaching (in their letters to the churches). The task of an elder or pastor is to study their writings, comparing them with the life, teachings and actions of Christ and the Old Testament Scriptures. On this basis they set forth the whole faith before the people of God and show its implications for their moral and spiritual lives.

To do this adequately is a full-time task and has led to the development of what today we call 'the full-time pastor'. There is no doubt this has been a great gift and blessing to the churches. Through devoting themselves to study, prayer and preaching some have been greatly used to bring people to the faith and build them up in the church. Some are being used in this way still and church members should see that this work is given a high priority in their church. Let them search for such men to minister to them. Then let them pray for them, support them, and above all pay attention to their preaching. This will ensure the health of their church, for God will honour it.

At the same time the other duties of elders should not be neglected. The one who is specializing in preaching and teaching is not able to perform all the tasks involved in 'supervision' – the personal counselling, the organization and administration of the church's affairs. These seem to increase as life becomes more complex. There has been a tendency to allow the New Testament's vision of a team of elders to lapse, to the great detriment of the churches and to the overburdening of the 'full-time pastor'. It is time the whole concept of leadership as outlined here were put into practice.

Do not forget about your commitments to the leaders. As well as their responsibilities to you, there are yours to them:

a) to recognize their calling, possibly even taking part in it, which is why you need to understand what elders are, how they are appointed and what qualities are required in them;

b) to co-operate with them, to respond to their ministry, which is why you need to know all this about their work;

c) above all to learn to trust them. They represent Christ to you! Trust them as you do him.

7
WHO ASSISTS THE ELDERS?

When we outlined the work of elders, did it strike you what a demanding job this is? They have not only to do the 'preaching and teaching' but 'direct the affairs of the church well' (1 Timothy 5:17).

The teaching aspect involves many hours of study and preparation in addition to the time actually devoted to the meetings and services. The supervising side of the work involves many more things: visiting the members or being visited by them; nurturing new believers with special sessions on their own, including preparation for baptism and membership; holding elders' meetings and implementing the decisions taken at them; holding members' meetings; delegating tasks and if necessary training people for them.

'Who is equal to such a task?' did I hear you say? Quite so. Divine help is indispensable. But they also need as much extraneous work taken off their hands as possible in order to be free to devote themselves to their particular calling.

To obviate this situation most churches have an office called 'deacon'. We find these in the New Testament, and the only times they are mentioned are in conjunction with 'elders' (Philippians 1:1; 1 Timothy 3:8). This in itself seems to indicate that the primary purpose of deacons was to assist the elders in the work of the local church.

In the early church it did not take the apostles long to discover that the demands of the church were so great they needed help, especially in the material care of the needy. So we find them asking the church for seven men to be set aside for this work (Acts 6). They were not 'deacons', although the word from which 'deacon' comes is found in verses 1 and 2 – the word meaning 'serve'. But in fact the history of deacons goes back much further. So first:

1. *How did deacons originate?*

A deacon is a servant of the needy and thus reflects the heart and nature of God himself. God has a special concern for the underprivileged, the weak and the vulnerable: he is 'a father to the fatherless, a defender of widows' (Psalm 68:5). He takes special interest in the poor and the sick and their care.

This is why, when he gave Israel his laws, God made special provision for such people. He did not undertake, however, to provide for them directly and miraculously, but required those who had sufficient to remember those less well-off. Read Exodus 22:22-27. This is only one of many passages in which the people are told to have a special regard for the deprived. The reason is always God's own regard for them: 'I am compassionate.' To break these laws was as culpable as to break any of the Ten Commandments.

In later centuries, after the Jews had been in exile, they no longer had liberty to govern themselves according to their God-given code. Nevertheless, this ministry was not altogether neglected. Extra-biblical writings tell us of the development of the local synagogue during this period. Every community had a synagogue, every synagogue had elders, and all elders were assisted by a *chazzan*, whose office was to collect alms from the people and distribute them among the needy.

Later, when Jesus came to teach the way of God perfectly, he included the duty of helping the poor in his doctrine (John 12:8) and in fact practised it himself (Acts 10:38).

Who assists the elders?

The early Christians followed his example from the beginning of the church. In fact, it was at the beginning that this problem was most acute. People who had come from all parts of the empire to Jerusalem for Pentecost became Christians and 'continued in the church'. They must soon have run out of travellers cheques! So they became dependent on the Christians who were already resident there. Since there were also widows and other needy people, the apostles were moved to call on the Christians to share their goods with those who lacked (Acts 2:44-45; 4:32-35). The distribution of all this needed to be carefully organized, but a lack of organization was causing inequalities as well as putting a strain on the spiritual ministry of the apostles. Rather than give up their special task of preaching, the apostles appointed certain men to take over the care of the needy (Acts 6).

This became a universal problem. Wherever churches were planted there were needy people. But there were also 'those able to help others' (1 Corinthians 12:28), those who had the desire to share and show kindness (Romans 12:8). It was from such that deacons eventually emerged.

2. What are deacons for?

Silly question! The secret is already out! Clearly their basic job is to see that the needy in the church are provided for. Of course this is the responsibility of every Christian who has sufficient for himself and his dependents, but it needs supervision and organization. Every one of us is to show 'mercy' (Romans 12:8), but it has to be organized or there will be injustice and neglect, as there was in the early days of the church until people were appointed to take charge of the matter.

On that occasion there were really two problems. One, that the apostles were having to neglect their ministry of preaching and leading worship in order to attend to the needy. They had to forsake the pulpit for 'serving at tables', that is, giving out the daily dole. If this had gone on, the church would have fallen apart, the converts would not have become established and people would not have been converted.

The other problem was that the responsibility of caring was not being properly discharged because the apostles did not have the necessary time to give it. A certain group of widows felt neglected, there was discontent and the threat of division. So the apostles handed it over to suitable men. After this, things went much better, as Acts 6:7 shows, where we see the beneficial effect on the spiritual as well as the material work of the church.

It could be argued that with our modern welfare state there is no more need for an elaborate system of providing for the needy. With the NHS, the DHSS, the DOE and all the other letters of the alphabet where does 'charity' come in? What is left for deacons to do? In spite of all this, they are still needed.

For one thing, there are certain situations that are not covered by the state. Its machinery is slow and cumbersome, not able to react quickly to emergencies. The church thus has a place in coming in quickly to meet short-term needs. Nor can all problems be solved with cash. The chronic sick, the old, the lonely and the depressed need not so much hand-outs as love, sympathy, friendship and counsel. The members of the church can provide these. Though it will often be done spontaneously by the members, it helps to have some specially devoted to this ministry, who will be on the look-out for needs and will have the means of meeting them at their disposal.

The other point is that there are in today's churches just as many jobs of which elders need to be relieved as there were in the first churches, if not more. Modern life is more mechanized and sophisticated. There is more administration and finance, more to do in looking after buildings. The 'helping' work of deacons is vital, if elders are going to be able to fulfil their essential ministry.

3. *How are deacons appointed?*

Deacons, like elders, are chosen by the local church. If you become a member of your church you will probably before long take part in the election of deacons. You need to know how to go about it. The main principle is to discern who among the members are most fitted for the work. Since we do not have the gift of discernment that was given to the apostles, we need some guiding principles. We find these in their writings, especially 1 Timothy 3:8-13. The main qualities we have to look for according to this passage are:

Godly character
They are to be 'worthy of respect' for their moral and spiritual integrity. They should be 'sincere' and true-hearted, lest they be tempted to show partiality to some rather than others. They should be self-disciplined, 'not indulging in much wine' (which does not mean total abstinence) and 'temperate' (vv.8,11). They may have to deal with malingerers and scroungers, so that they will need a wise and cool head! They should be honest and trustworthy, 'not pursuing dishonest gain'. They are handling others' money, in fact the Lord's money.

Soundness in the faith (v.9)
Although not normally called on to teach and preach, they are representatives of the church and assistants to those who do teach. It is important for deacons to be one in faith with elders. Where there is disagreement on basic principles things will soon go wrong in practice. They must be

like-minded with their elders and have a desire to promote the gospel, even if they are not as directly involved as elders. If the local church has a basis of doctrine, deacons should be able to subscribe to it.

Good managerial ability (v.12)

The work of deacons calls for administration and organization, and the ability to handle people. They prove their capability in this direction by the way they conduct their family life: how they relate to their wives, control their children and manage their home. If they cannot do this they cannot manage God's 'household'. If they prove competent here they are likely to be good deacons.

Sympathy

Romans 12:8 (which is all about sympathy) does not specifically refer to deacons, because obviously all Christians should have this quality and express it in the ways mentioned in that verse. But deacons should be noted for these things: generosity, diligence, mercy and cheerfulness. A good deacon is not one who is merely efficient in the work of administration and organization. He is dealing with people who need encouraging as well as organizing. He should not be a cold, faceless bureaucrat, but one who gives himself and his time willingly.

Paul tells us to take care in examining people for their suitability to be deacons (v.10). We should not be in a hurry to appoint people who appear to be above the others because they are business or 'professional' people. Although such people usually have a good deal to offer, they may lack some of the qualities which are even more important. They must be examined on these before being allowed to 'serve as deacons'.

4. How many deacons should a church have? For how long should they serve?

Some churches have a fixed number, but this is probably not the best way. It is better to decide what areas of church life need special supervision and appoint a number accordingly. Usually a secretary and treasurer are needed. Sometimes it is desirable to have someone to supervise the maintenance of the buildings, and it is good to have someone in charge of publicity, literature and so on. Deacons can be appointed for these purposes. It is not good to have people as deacons who have no particular responsibility, as it creates love of office, title and power, which can lead to problems.

As regards length of service, there is no rule in Scripture for this either. While a deacon is able and willing to do a particular job, and while that job is still needed, he should be allowed to continue in office. There is no point in changing personnel every so often for the sake of it. If a deacon is inefficient or falls ill, or loses interest, then is the time for a change.

To have people bearing the title of 'deacon' is not important in itself. What matters is that the necessary work of the church is attended to. When this is done it ensures that the elders are not burdened or distracted from their tasks. The great aim is that the members of the church are served and Christ is glorified.

8
HOW DOES CHURCH MEMBERSHIP END?

To talk about ending your membership before you have begun it is like asking your friend who has just arrived what time he's going to leave! However, the matter is going to crop up in some way or other – if not for yourself then for someone else in the fellowship. Every church member needs to know how to handle this question biblically. Apart from death (which is not so much an ending of membership as a promotion from the church militant to the church triumphant), Scripture and common sense indicate three ways in which membership in a particular church comes to an end.

1. *By transfer or commendation*

In New Testament times people were far less mobile than they are today. Nevertheless from time to time Christians travelled to other towns or countries. When this happened we sometimes read of their being 'commended' to the church in the place they moved to. For example, an Alexandrian Jew called Apollos spent some time in Ephesus where his somewhat defective understanding of Christianity was deepened by coming into contact with a Christian couple, Priscilla and Aquila. After a time he moved on to Corinth and 'the brothers . . . wrote to the disciples there to welcome him' (Acts 18:27). He was 'commended' from the church in Ephesus to the church in Corinth. Also there was Phoebe who belonged to the church in Cenchrea near Corinth. She went to Rome and

How does church membership end?

was commended to the church by no less a person than the apostle Paul (Romans 16:1-2).

Today many more Christians move around, usually on account of employment. Supposing this happens to you, what do you do? Unless there are good reasons you should attend the nearest evangelical church to your new home. But what about your membership? Do not do what some Christians do and remain on the roll of your former church. This is often done for sentimental reasons or sometimes just neglected, which is not in accord with the Bible's teaching on the church. On the other hand don't resign and start again from square one in the new church. Ask your former church to commend you to the new one as a member in good standing. The leadership of the new church should then liaise with that of your former church with a view to your being received in a simple way without having to be re-examined or pass through an elaborate procedure. Independent evangelical churches would be greatly improved if they could establish the principle that those who are acceptable in one church should be equally acceptable in another. Is not the real basis of membership not our written constitutions but that Christ has received us (Romans 15:7)? Why should one church require more than another?

2. *By release from commitments*

Let us suppose a very different scenario, in fact, a tragic one. After a period of time you undergo a change of mind or heart. At the time of joining you sincerely want to commit yourself to the people, the teachings and the work of the church. If all goes well this commitment increases as you learn more and become more deeply involved. This is what usually happens and you can and should expect it in your own case.

I want to be a church member

Alas, this is not always so. Sometimes a member discovers he or she does not after all share the convictions of the church. He came in with a limited understanding of Christianity and finds as he goes on that there are certain aspects he cannot accept, try as he will – perhaps man's state of sin, certain attributes of God, the inerrancy of Scripture or some other vital truth. Or possibly he accepted these at first and then for some reason came to change his views on them, to see things in a different way. Perhaps his own spiritual life goes into a decline and he loses interest in prayer, worship, Bible reading and preaching. And this goes on and on, getting worse and worse, so that he never enjoys any aspect of spiritual life, private or corporate. In other words, he finds himself unable to fulfil the commitments he undertook on joining the church.

Supposing something like this happens to you; or to someone in your church, so that you along with others have to decide how to meet this state of affairs. How should it be handled?

First of all, do not just write a letter of resignation and then be seen no more. Resigning is against the New Testament concept of the church as a body and a family. It is an open breach of fellowship and harms everyone, especially the church. It is a kind of vote of censure. There may, of course, be situations which call for this censure. If it is the *church* that goes astray and introduces teachings or practices contrary to the gospel, or if its minister does so and is not brought to book, then probably resigning is the only course.

But some Christians resign over a dispute with another member, or because they disapprove of the pastor. They do not like his preaching, object to some practice he has introduced, or to his stopping of some cherished activity. Very often it is just a personal dislike. Sometimes they resign because they do not get their way in a church meeting when matters to do with worship or the buildings are raised. Sometimes a combination of events makes them feel generally disaffected with the whole set-up. So they resign.

None of these is a resigning issue. It is possible to resolve any of them, provided there is communication between the parties concerned and the problems are discussed in a spirit of love and humility. Where all concerned have as their greatest desire the truth and unity of their church, not their own feelings or wishes, then these things will be settled without resignations.

But the case we are considering is different. Of course the problems which have led to it should be shared as fully as possible. If you do have doubts and questions about the church's doctrine, then raise them with a friend or leader. Or if your views do change do not be afraid or ashamed to say so, and to share it with someone. If your spiritual life goes into a decline, do not wait until it so bad that people begin to notice, only to find that it is too late to save it. Go to someone, ask for prayer and counsel. Like most diseases, spiritual sickness can be cured if it is diagnosed early enough.

But if all possible efforts to achieve a cure have been made, and failed, what then? Although Scripture does not give us specific guidance, its general principles of humility, forbearance, love and unity would seem to suggest that the least painful way of dealing with this condition is for you to request to be released from the ties of membership and for the church to agree on this. You would approach someone, probably the pastor, with this request, and he would share it with the officers and possibly the other members. Then he would come back to you informing you that your request had been granted.

In this way you and the church would at least part ami-

I want to be a church member

cably. You would not hold any resentment against them or they against you. You and they would be able to keep in touch. If you go off in a huff or they demand your resignation, then any subsequent restoration is made more difficult. But an agreement to release does leave the door open should there be a further change of heart in you. The same applies if the person concerned is not yourself but someone else in the fellowship. If you have thought through this section of our study beforehand then you will know how to proceed should the situation arise.

3. By church discipline or excommunication

This is the most serious and tragic of the ways in which church membership may end. For it happens, not through changes in circumstances, nor through an unsought change of heart and mind, but through a deliberate change of conduct. The New Testament indicates that there are certain kinds of misbehaviour in Christians which are so serious that they bring the church, the gospel and the name of Christ into disrepute. If the offender, after clear warnings, fails to put things right he has to be dismissed from the church.

The New Testament is much clearer on what these acts of misbehaviour are and how to deal with them than it is on the first two situations we have discussed. You who are in process of becoming a member will not be contemplating the possibility of anything like this. Nevertheless it may happen that someone in your church falls and the church of which you are a part is called on to consider the exercise of discipline. So you need to be prepared. You need also to remember that the devil is subtle and can catch you off guard. Paul warned those Galatian Christians who had not fallen into error to deal gently with offenders and 'watch yourself, or you also may be tempted' (Galatians 6:1).

How does church membership end?

Unresolved disputes

At this point you will need to refer to Matthew 18:15-18. Christians are human and like other people they can fall out with each other. Where this happens the offended party should draw the attention of the offender to his fault and hope for an apology. If it is forthcoming he should forgive and all will be well (see Luke 17:1-4). Jesus regarded this as such a serious matter that he taught that all disputes should be put right before the parties next attended public worship (Matthew 5:23-24).

In the last two passages mentioned the Lord did not go into detail as to *how* to settle grievances, nor what to do if attempts at reconciliation fail. All this is made clear in Matthew 18:15-18. This is something you really need to know, for situations like this are bound to arise – between you and a fellow Christian and between others in your church. There are four steps:

(i) (v.15). This is similar to the other two passages: that is, if someone wrongs you, you should point this out and expect an apology. At this stage no one else should be involved. You do not bring anyone else in, either friend or church officer. If it is settled in this way, no one else will be the wiser and that is the best thing; there will be no gossip. But supposing the other will not admit his fault or apologize, what then? Then you proceed to:

(ii) (v.16). At this point others begin to get involved. You ask two or three trusted friends to come with you when you make a renewed attempt at reconciliation. The quotation from Deuteronomy 19:15 indicates the main purpose of bringing in these friends – to act as witnesses. They are not taking sides and making it three or four against one. They are there to 'see fair play', to witness to the fact that you are making a genuine attempt to put things right in Christ's appointed way. For the matter may have to be taken further, in which case they will be available with the evidence. Nevertheless they are not just silent observers. Since v.17 accuses the offender of not listening to them, they obviously say something – presumably pointing out to the offender his Christian duty of admitting his fault and apologizing. Perhaps they quote Luke 17:1-4 or Matthew 5:23-24. But let us suppose, as v.17 says, that he 'refuses to listen to them'. What then?

(iii) (v.17). Now the whole church becomes involved. The elders or pastor will be informed of the situation and the two or three witnesses will verify the offender's obduracy. The elders will attempt to persuade him to apologize and warn him of the serious consequences of not doing so (which we will come to in a moment). If the elders fail, they will raise the matter at a church meeting. They will ask the church for a unanimous voice in calling for repentance and will convey this to the offender. Normally this will be sufficient. Who will remain obdurate with all his Christian brothers and sisters against him, threatening his exclusion from the fellowship? Only someone whose heart is so hard that he must have fallen into the hands of Satan. So should this fail, we proceed to:

(iv) (v.17). Our Lord is using Jewish terminology at this point because his disciples were all Jews at that time; the work of redemption was not complete nor was the Spirit given. To the Jew a 'pagan' stood outside the covenant of God, and a 'tax collector', although a Jew by birth, had gone over to the enemy, he was serving the Romans, he was a traitor. Translated into Christian language the meaning is that an obdurate person is to be treated as if he were a non-Christian, or worse – a traitor in the camp, a 'mole', an enemy agent, a servant of Satan. In practice this means that such a person is not welcome in gatherings for Christian fellowship, worship and ministry, particularly the Lord's Supper and church meetings.

If this sounds terrible that is because it is terrible. It is rarely necessary to go to this point if the first three steps are taken. Where things are not nipped in the bud and proceeded with calmly and sensibly, it is more likely to come to sterner measures. This is why it is so important for every member to know the procedure and follow it.

Division over doctrine

Now read Romans 16:17-20. Imagine a situation in which you or some other member began to entertain a teaching which goes contrary to the gospel. This is not the same as the situation we considered in the second section of this chapter. For one thing, it is not a merely negative attitude in which doubts arise about the doctrines held by the church. It is more positive in the sense that you embrace some new teaching that is abroad, a new interpretation of Christianity, or a cult.

For another thing, you do not just keep it to yourself or go away on your own to cherish it. You spread it around, you persuade others about it and gather a party around you. This is what is really meant by 'heresy'. A heretic is not someone who only privately disbelieves the doctrines of the gospel and holds some alternative view. A local church should be strong enough to take such people on board until such time as they either feel a change of wind or voluntarily abandon ship. A heretic is one who publicly proclaims his doctrine, leads others astray and thus divides the church, as Paul says in Romans 16.

This is the really serious thing. Church members are not expected to go witch-hunting for people with doctrinal aberrations, nor to report to the authorities every doctrinal difficulty someone might express. Such things can be

I want to be a church member

looked into, discussed and resolved amicably without dividing the church. The serious aspect of this is the creation of division over doctrine. The apostles referred to it on several other occasions: 1 Timothy 6:3-5; Titus 3:10-11; 2 John 7-10.

It is where this occurs that severe discipline must be applied. The elders will be informed (indeed will probably be among the first to be aware of it), will investigate and issue warnings. If these have no success, they will have to proceed to excommunicate, as described in Matthew 18:17.

Immoral behaviour

Here you need to read 1 Corinthians 5. It is not only breaches of fellowship and doctrine that call for discipline but also of conduct. Behaviour that is so bad it causes scandal outside the church has to be dealt with. This was what happened in Corinth – there was sexual sin of a kind that was unacceptable even in decadent Corinth, which is saying a lot.

Paul says in verse 3 that had he been physically present he would have dealt with it himself by virtue of his apostolic authority. Since he was absent the church had the authority, in fact the responsibility, to deal with it. This they must do firmly and without delay by the exclusion of the offender from the fellowship (vv. 2,7,10-13).

The difficult verse 5 probably needs to be understood in this context. Someone who is treated like a 'pagan' (Matthew 18:17) is placed outside the Lord's protection; he is a sheep away from the fold and the care of the shepherd, exposed to the elements and to wild beasts. He returns to the domain of Satan. But he does so under divine judgment, which may take the form of sickness or even death. This was actually happening in the Corinthian church (11:29-30). It happened in Jerusalem with Ananias and

Sapphira who 'lied to the Holy Spirit' and fell dead at the word of the apostle Peter (Acts 5:1-11).

While our churches and their leaders do not have such awesome power now, this does teach us the seriousness of flagrant misconduct on the part of church members and the possible consequences of non-repentance.

Nor are we confined to the teachings of Paul in the matter. In Revelation 2 the glorified Christ himself communicates with the churches of Ephesus, Pergamum and Thyatira through John. He censures those who follow the teaching of Nicolas, which he describes as 'the teaching of Balaam' or of 'Jezebel'. This was probably a form of permissiveness, a teaching that it was acceptable for converts from paganism to continue to practise idolatry in the form of religious fornication by visiting temple prostitutes. Christ says that if the churches do not deal with this he will.

This indicates what happens where churches fail to exercise discipline in serious situations. God himself takes over the discipline, as he did in Corinth (1 Corinthians 11:31-32). Painful as it is, discipline is a necessary purging of the body of Christ (5:7-8), from which they emerge purified. Not only do they flush out the foreign body which is causing the spiritual sickness, but they actually inflict a defeat on Satan (Romans 16:20).

Unpleasant reading as all this is, it is essential for all church members. Fire warnings and details of nuclear attacks make unpleasant reading, but they are better than being caught unawares with no fire-fighting equipment or nuclear shelter. We have to face reality. In your present state of euphoria about the Christian life you may think all this is a scare story. But the apostles had much experience of what really happens in churches when Satan gets a foothold. We must be on the look-out for him. We must know all about his schemes and how to combat them.

9
IS THERE LIFE OUTSIDE THE LOCAL CHURCH?

Earlier in our studies we looked at four pictures which the New Testament uses to describe the church. Actually there is a fifth one: the kingdom. The reason for not including it in that section was because in no way can the kingdom be regarded as a description of a *local* church. It is not even agreed that it is right to equate it with the *universal* church. Many who have done so have abused it by making it support their erroneous ideas. The Roman Catholic Church uses it to justify the temporal power of the Pope – the view that as 'Vicar of Christ' he is head of nations as well as of the church. This is symbolized in his triple tiara. Some Protestants have used it to justify the 'social gospel' – the idea that the church exists to set up a utopian socialist-type society which, when achieved will be 'the kingdom of God'. We have to reject this, not least because Jesus said, 'My kingdom is not of this world' (John 18:36). That means his church does not have political power or use political methods. It influences the world not by direct rule but through the truth of its message, the witness of its members' lives and the power of its prayers.

Even with these safeguards it would still not be accurate to see the church and the kingdom referring to one and the same thing. The kingdom is a broader concept because it describes the whole compass of God's sovereign rule, including the unbelieving world, the material universe and the supernatural realm, over all of which God reigns. However, the same Christ who is 'head over everything' (Ephesians 1:21-22) is head of the church (4:15). He rules it as its King, although in a different way from the way he reigns over the other spheres.

The 'kingdom of God' is the New Testament counterpart of 'the kingdom of Israel', that nation whose true King was God. Israel was a 'theocracy' – God made all its laws and appointed its officials (Isaiah 33:22). He called out its armies and gave them victory or defeat. This kingdom was brought to an end when the Jews rejected their Messiah: 'the kingdom of God will be taken away from you and given to a people who will produce its fruit' (Matthew 21:43). It was replaced with one so much more glorious that it could be called 'the kingdom of heaven', that is, heaven on earth. This was to comprise people of all nations who through the gospel submitted to God's chosen Messiah. Faith in Christ would bring them into the sphere of his personal rule, his kingdom, and thus at the same time into his church.

When Peter and the apostles came to this faith Jesus declared them the first stones in his building, his church; and then said he would give them 'the keys of the kingdom' (Matthew 16:19). This shows that there is a certain correspondence between the two ideas. Those who through the preaching of the apostolic gospel are brought into the kingdom are also admitted to the church, where Christ particularly exercises his sovereign rule. Gentiles are equally welcome, for when they come to Christ they are made 'fellow-citizens with God's people' (Ephesians 2:19), they belong to the same 'city-state' (as Greeks and Romans would have understood this language). At the same time they are 'built' into Christ's 'holy temple', the church (vv. 20-22). So Christians belong both to the church and the kingdom.

It is very important that you as a potential member of a local church understand this teaching on the kingdom as clearly as you understand the other aspects. You need to realize that while you belong in a special sense to the Christians with whom you meet regularly you also belong to all other Christians. Some Christians have no conception of this. They may be very loyal members of their local church, yet they feel nothing for Christians elsewhere, they never meet with Christians from other churches and take no interest in what is happening to Christians nationwide and worldwide. They have grasped the teaching of the New Testament on the local church and found it enough for them. But of its teaching on the universal church they are totally ignorant.

This teaching is contained in the idea of 'the kingdom'. Christ unlocks to us the door not just of the local church but of his whole kingdom. We are 'fellow-citizens with God's people' – *all* God's people. We are like people who hail from the same country, honour the same flag, speak the same language, abide by the same laws, use the same currency, fight the same wars and so on. Christians of all towns and villages, all countries and continents, belong to us. Christ said that the kingdom belongs to the members of the church: 'Do not be afraid, little flock, for your Father has been pleased to give you the kingdom' (Luke 12:32). Believers in Jesus are his sheep, the members of his flock, the church. It is to his sheep, the members of his church, that he gives the kingdom.

We must have a broad outlook. Some Christians are so narrow-minded they cannot see beyond their own relationship with Christ. They are complete individualists, they will not even join the local church. Let us hope you are not going down their road and that you have seen that an individual Christian, while complete in Christ, is also a limb or organ of his body, the local church. The other Christians in your church belong to you and you to them, as you belong to Christ and he to you. But don't stop there. Other local churches and their members belong to you and you

Is there life outside the local church?

to them – right throughout the world. When you have an opportunity meet with other Christians, get together with other churches to encourage and build each other up, to help the young, to co-operate in evangelism, to promote missionary work or confront your locality or the nation with some moral or social issue which has cropped up. We are all on the same side. We are all the kingdom of Christ and those outside him are the kingdom of this world, the domain of Satan. We need each other's encouragement, support and prayer in this great conflict.

But don't stop there either! It is not only the churches and their members now living who belong to you, but churches and their members from the past. Even though long dead they still live in the 'church triumphant'. Their example and victory can inspire the 'church militant', as athletes who have completed their event cheer on those still competing (Hebrews 12:1). So read the exploits of Christians from the past and their leaders: the missionaries of the last two centuries, the Victorian social reformers, the eighteenth-century revivalists, the seventeenth-century Puritans, the sixteenth-century Reformers, the pre-Reformation lonely lights, such as Wycliffe and Hus. Go back further to the British and continental missionaries of the early centuries: Boniface, Columba, Patrick and Aidan. Then go back to the first four centuries, the persecuted church, until you reach the first century, the apostolic age – the acts of the apostles themselves and their fellow believers. They are all yours – 'whether Paul or Apollos or Cephas [Peter]' (1 Corinthians 3:22).

Don't stop there! There was a church before the time of Jesus: Israel was the church of the old covenant – the people of God, his flock and family. It was formed at the foot of Mount Sinai, when God entered into covenant with them as 'a kingdom of priests and a holy nation' (Exodus 19:6). This was 'the assembly [church] in the desert' referred to

I want to be a church member

by Stephen (Acts 7:38). That church too belongs to you, it is part of God's kingdom. Its leader, Moses, belongs to you, as does its founder, Abraham, along with the other patriarchs and the successors of Moses: Joshua, the judges, David and the other kings, the prophets and priests. They live still, for God 'is not the God of the dead but of the living' (Matthew 22:32). Have fellowship with them! See them and hear them cheering you on! They are yours: 'You have come to Mount Zion, to the heavenly Jerusalem, the city of the living God . . . to the church of the first-born, whose names are written in heaven . . . to the spirits of righteous men made perfect' (Hebrews 12:22-23).

Then look in the other direction, to the future. As you grow old and die others will replace you so that your church will go on. Those future members are yours too! However long this age lasts and however many more millions are brought into the kingdom, they are all yours: the present and the future are yours because 'you are of Christ, and Christ is of God' (1 Corinthians 3:22-23).

The church in heaven is yours too – not only as it is now but as it will be when it is complete, when every room in the mansion is filled and every place at the Lamb's banqueting table occupied. You have a reserved seat there if your name is 'written in the Lamb's book of life' (Revelation 21:27). You have a room in the Father's house prepared for you to take up when he comes back (John 14:2-3). You have a home in the heavenly city, the new Jerusalem which he is preparing (Revelation 21:2). There will be gathered that 'great multitude that no-one could count' (7:9). It will consist of believers from the old dispensation, represented by the twelve gates bearing the names of the twelve tribes of Israel (21:12), and those of the present age, represented by the twelve foundation stones bearing the names of the twelve apostles (21:14). You are part of that now by faith and hope. It belongs to you, it is promised. Your original

To Bala for a Bible by Elisabeth Williams. The true story of Mary Jones and the beginnings of the Bible Society.

The Welsh Revival of 1904 by Eifion Evans. A thorough but readable study of the 1904 Revival. Foreword by D.M. Lloyd-Jones.

Revival Comes to Wales by Eifion Evans. A moving and thrilling account of the mighty working of God the Holy Spirit in Wales at the time of the 1859 Revival.

Two Welsh Revivalists by Eifion Evans. The fascinating stories of Humphrey Jones and Dafydd Morgan, the two prominent leaders during the 1859 Revival in Wales.

Howell Harris and the Dawn of Revival by Richard Bennett; introduction by D.M. Lloyd-Jones. A study of the early spiritual life of Howell Harris and the beginnings of the Great Awakening of the eighteenth century in Wales.

'Excuse Me, Mr Davies – Hallelujah!' by Geraint D. Fielder; foreword by Lady Catherwood. The absorbing story of evangelical student witness in Wales in the twentieth century, a story which includes periods of quite remarkable spiritual blessing.

Christian Family Matters edited by Ian Shaw, foreword by Sir Frederick Catherwood. Clear biblical guidelines by experienced contributors on such matters as marriage, parenthood, divorce and adoption.

Social Issues and the Local Church edited by Ian Shaw. Subjects covered include the state, work, education, mission, social welfare and the role of women in the local church.

The Christian Heritage of Welsh Education by R.M. Jones & Gwyn Davies. A bird's-eye view of Christian education in Wales down the centuries which demonstrates its close inter-relationship with revival.

An Angry God? by Eryl Davies. What the Bible says about the wrath of God, final judgment and hell.

Gospel and Church by Hywel R. Jones. An evangelical evaluation of ecumenical documents on church unity.

Christian Hymns edited by Paul E. G. Cook and Graham Harrison. A comprehensive selection of 901 hymns. The editions available include a large-type words edition. A lineal index and concordance is also available.

Christian Hymn-writers by Elsie Houghton. Brief biographies of great hymn-writers through the ages.

The Evangelical Magazine of Wales. A bimonthly magazine with a wide range of articles on all aspects of Christian faith and life.

Books for the earnest seeker and the new Christian

by Peter Jeffery

I Will Never Become a Christian – carefully and convincingly dismantles the reasons and excuses given by the convinced unbeliever and includes some remarkable testimonies of believers who once said 'I will never become a Christian!'

Seeking God – a clear explanation of the gospel, written for the earnest seeker after faith.

All Things New – a help for those beginning the Christian life.

Walk Worthy – a sequel to *All Things New*, setting out to present clear guidelines on issues with which the new Christian will have to grapple during the early years after conversion.

Firm Foundations (with Owen Milton) – a two-month Bible-reading course introducing readers to 62 key chapters of the Bible and to some of the most important teachings of the Word of God.

Stand Firm – a young Christian's guide to the armour of God.

Christian Handbook – a straightforward guide to the Bible, church history and Christian doctrine. Available in hardback and paperback.